PORTRAIT OF LEEDS

OTHER *PORTRAIT* BOOKS

Portrait of
LEEDS

BRIAN THOMPSON

ROBERT HALE · LONDON

© Brian Thompson 1971
First published in Great Britain 1971

ISBN 0 7091 2773 1

Robert Hale & Company
63 Old Brompton Road
London S.W.7

PRINTED IN GREAT BRITAIN
BY EBENEZER BAYLIS AND SON LTD.
THE TRINITY PRESS, WORCESTER, AND LONDON

CONTENTS

ILLUSTRATIONS

To my mother and father

PREFACE

I was first attracted to Leeds some ten or more years ago for all those big-city qualities which reminded me of my own birthplace in working-class London. There is an urban landscape that is just as powerful as "an impulse from a vernal wood" in teaching of man, of moral evil and of good. Wordsworth was not a great poet of cities but of the open spaces and the solitary figures in them. He may have missed that strong sentimental bond that ties city folk to their landscape and the dense peopling of street after street, as far as the eye stretches. As I have tried to explain in the section of this book that deals with Hunslet, no one who has grown up in the streets can ever shake the power the red, grey and black landscape has on their imagination. For these people, walking in the street at dusk, with the weary yellows and oranges of street-lighting clocking-on, is like coming home.

Leeds is that kind of home for me, although not my home. There are many, many people who can write a more personal record of the city, and many who can write a more scholarly history of Leeds. I have tried to hold close to the affection I feel for all large towns and cities and to write of those things in Leeds that are a matter of observation, or are questions which simple observation poses. I have had the help of a great tradition of amateur scholarship and interest that expresses itself in correspondence to local papers, membership of adult education classes, publications and learned societies. In addition to these many there are many more again in pubs and shops, market-stalls and 'bus shelters who seem to be waiting only the opportunity to say something original or unexpected about their particular map of Leeds.

For their particular help and encouragement I should like to

thank Richard Copley for many helpful suggestions; Louis
Teeman for invaluable information about the early history of
Jews in Leeds; the libraries of the City, the Leeds Library and the
Thoresby Society; Mrs. Mary Ness for her help with a difficult
manuscript; and the friends who were good enough to listen to
parts of the book which struck me as being particularly relevant.
Those of them born in Leeds probably noticed as young children
what impressed me as a grown man: they were kind enough not
to say so. Finally, I should like to thank my wife and children for
their encouragement of any common sense this book may contain.

Leeds   B.T.

I

"A BUSY, WEALTHY AND POPULOUS TOWN . . ."

FROM the south, the railway brings you into Leeds by a shallow curve, the line running along embankments and over bridges. If you are riding the London train, your fellow-passengers will judge exactly when to stand up and reach for their cases, from small marks of landscape you perhaps may miss. Then, quite suddenly, the tracks curve round and you can see the city rising gradually on the north bank of the Aire, the skyline dominated by the university only because it is in the lightest stone. As you look more closely, the scene is bulky with big buildings. There seem to be as many church spires as factory chimneys. You have time to note several new multi-storey buildings, before your eye is distracted by Leeds's most characteristic sight—a steep sea of modest, regular, orderly streets, not much more than a hundred years old. You first recognize the size of this great industrial city not by its factories and works, but by the houses of the ordinary people.

Leeds City Station has been newly rebuilt. Taking your cue from the returning businessmen, you fetch your case from the rack, seeing out of the corner of your eye the curious contradictory signs of an industrial community. At the end of a street of back-to-backs a horse is tethered on a tiny patch of grass. Across the way a woman draws the curtains on her sleeping children; her house at the very gates of a great engine shed. A new-model car is parked on a lot beside the empty shells of old wrecks. An old man walks slowly towards the corner pub. Then, abruptly, you are into the new station, built over the old, at the very banks of the river. If you are a passenger from the London train, you will

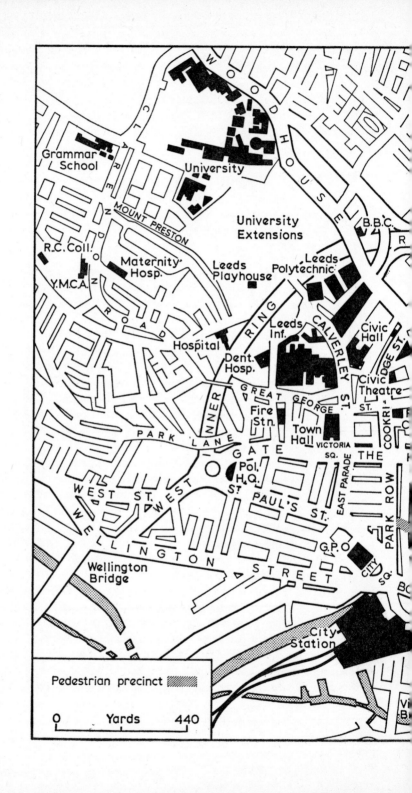

Pedestrian precinct

0   Yards   440

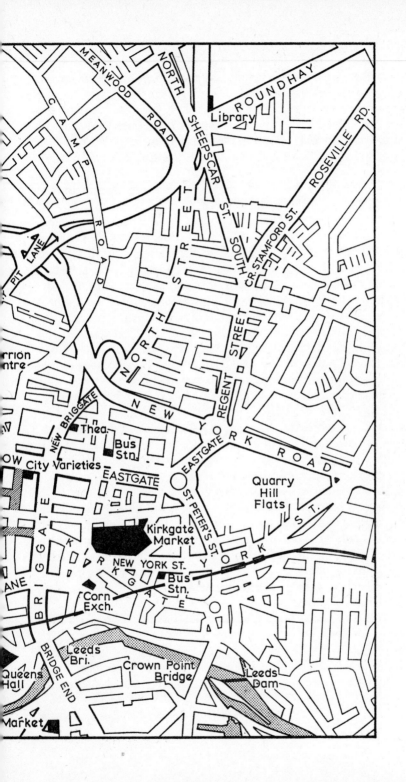

most likely need to cross the lines by an underground passageway. You would not be in Leeds if you did not hear at least one grumble about these station steps. Although the new station has been in operation for years, Leeds took a jaundiced view of the improvements and it is not in the nature of the city to take things as they come. The station steps are a topic still good for a drink in most pubs.

To a Leeds citizen, Leeds is the best place in the world, bar none. He does not have the easy feeling of propriety they have at the other end of the line, in London. Neither is he as careless. What is good in Leeds has been hard won and is jealously guarded. What is bad is fiercely debated. Sometimes, to an outsider, Leeds pride can seem impractical and even foolhardy. To a certain extent, this whole book is about just that particular kind of pride. Most Northern cities have it and it is what makes the North worth living in: it is one of the few things a Northerner takes for granted. His town, his city and—above all in Yorkshire—his county is the best place in the world, bar none. Nobody has ever compared Leeds with Venice. That is only because nobody has thought it worth the bother. Leeds is bound to be better.

Defoe came to Leeds in 1725 and found it "a large, wealthy and populous town". He was particularly impressed by the cloth market, of which he leaves a good account. Twice a week, between seven and nine in the morning, the small clothiers carried a piece of their work to stalls set out in Briggate, which runs north from the river up a gentle hill. Defoe was impressed by the order and discipline of the market as well as by the size of its dealings. Yorkshire cloth was the cheapest and most serviceable in the land. In addition to the hungry home market, a piece of Leeds cloth would find its way to America, Russia, Sweden and to anywhere in Germany. Defoe describes the merchants at market with pattern books sent on from the continental agents, holding the swatches to the cloth they saw before them, matching up colour and texture.

A great deal has been written of English social life before the Industrial Revolution. People who lived through it hark back inevitably to the halcyon days of their childhood, when it had been in their imagination a perpetual summer. Their chief recollection is most often of a sturdy independence, which the factory

Leeds Town Hall—the tower, a brilliant afterthought

system and the machine necessarily destroyed. In the eighteenth century there can have been few places in England more prosperous and with as much security as the woollen districts of the West Riding. The clothiers Defoe saw selling their goods abroad were almost all small men; independent, hard-working and in a general sense protected. In the manufacture of woollens, they had centuries of expertise behind them. As the century wore on, they took a larger and larger share of the worsted trade away from the West Country and East Anglia. They did not distinguish between master and hand.

Woollens and worsteds were a national industry worked by the domestic system. The picture is an attractive one, of women carrying their spinning wheels into the sun on a fine day, of tenters' fields heavy with cloth, of the fulling mills at every suitable stream. In the evenings, the men sat at single looms, each cottage alive with the soft clack-clack of their weaving. In the very early morning, the long walk to market with a piece of cloth likely to find its way anywhere in the kingdom, or as far afield as the American colonies.

At first sight, such a picture seems hard to fit to Leeds as it is today. There seems nothing left, nothing of the spirit of quiet, attentive work in small groups, always close to water, always close to the open fields. One of Leeds's greatest biographers, Edward Baines, writing in 1870, still identified the old domestic manufacturers, but only to record their final passing. What happened to Leeds in the nineteenth century was what made it into a city. The Industrial Revolution made this city into the fifth largest in England. Without writing a straightforward history of the place, one must nevertheless come again and again to the sudden, staggering and colossal events of the past. For ordinary families, the change has been infinitely more important than a continuous world war. Leeds, like other cities, but with its own story to tell, has lived through a revolution, and has now to face another. This is a portrait of that condition and the people whose experience of life it is.

The West Riding of Yorkshire is one of the largest administrative areas of Great Britain. The railway line to Scotland runs well to the east, through York. The Great North Road lies a little farther west, but does little more than square off the eastern

2

The Saxon Porch of Adel Church

edges of the administrative map. The really vital features of this beautiful, surprising, and amazingly various county are the west-east rivers, giving deep and broad valleys in the south and the incomparable Dales to the north.

In the centre of the picture is the massive concentration of population about Leeds and Bradford. Leeds stands on the River Aire, about equidistant from each coast and halfway between London and Edinburgh. The Aire can be navigated to the Humber estuary. By canal, Leeds was connected to Liverpool in the great heyday of commercial expansion. Water gave it its first advantage: in Yorkshire you still think across the country, following the river course. That is how the population is disposed; and the great recreational areas of the county extol the same geographical feature. In Yorkshire you climb a hill to look into a valley.

Leeds is a working city and the Aire is a working river. There are no parks and gardens sweeping down to a pleasant prospect of swans and swings, boating and riverside picnics. A Yorkshireman once visited Dublin and was asked if he had ever seen a wider river than the Liffey. When he said mildly enough that he thought the Thames at London to be wider, the Irishman thought for a moment and then said, "Now, if the river was any wider, where would you find room for all the houses on the banks?" The Aire is like that. A bus depot crowds in among the old wharves. The City Station is at the water's edge. Upstream of the weir, the river creeps through the city unnoticed. At any one time there might be a few students sketching or a party of industrial historians making their way along the wharves or in among the locks. Half-close the eye, and one can see it as it was, with the carts rolling under brake down Briggate, the hoists at work over the holds of the barges, a scene alive with men and horses and sail and steam. Even in those days, a difficult place to meander, because of the work done there, the business transacted—but vital and lively, the noisiest, possibly the most dangerous place in Leeds.

To the north of the river the land rises. Becks have cut their own paths to the mainstream: the land rises and falls as it is traversed. But get on to the hog's back at Sheepscar and you rise fast and straight for Harrogate. Within a ten-minute drive, you are in among the sheep. The grass is as green as you will find anywhere in England. The villages are as smart and prosperous as any, and the air as clear. You are running across the natural lie of the land by going north, heading towards the countryside depopulated by the sudden expansion of the factory towns. In Yorkshire an open space is not just a planning provision (as it might be in the Home Counties); it has a history to it formed by the sucking action of the valley towns. The busiest time on many of these roads north is at the weekend, when the great-grandsons of the spinners, the weavers and the knitters go back for a ride round their forsaken inheritance.

But to the south of the river the land is flatter, more featureless. The coalfields run up and under Leeds's boundary. A different people, with their own history, live to the south; something that is recognized, inherited, cherished. Although Leeds is a city of half a million people with as many amenities as a place that size deserves (or almost as many), the population to the south of the river is tugged south, to sturdy towns much smaller than Leeds— to Wakefield, to Barnsley, ultimately to Sheffield. Their sense of locality does not depend on Leeds as a marker. In unbroken tenancy of a house, or a few acres of land, or a trade, many of them can claim a longer record than most Leeds folk. They generally do.

The most interesting geographical feature, and the one hardest to describe, is the relationship of Leeds to its western neighbours, in particular Bradford. Here are two great towns ten miles apart, literally shoulder to shoulder, apparently much the same in outlook and background. What keeps them apart? They are like two Japanese sharing one seat—occupying much the same space but completely contained and independent. From the beer to the government Leeds and Bradford are separate and unlike. The only thing they have been known to share is the airport, which is a sort of neutral ground between them. They have different accents. Each claims for the other a different (and identically unflattering) character. They are said not to think in the same ways, like the same things, believe in the same truths.

Somehow or other the independence Leeds has of its rich neighbour Bradford holds the key to its character. Leeds has crowded a lot of history and a great number of people into the last 150 years of its life. For all sorts of reasons, all of them fascinating, not all of them consciously recorded, it has leapt from a secure knowledge of what it is to a much less certain idea of what it may become.

It is almost as though Leeds were in essence an unfinished city, overrun by events. There is one particular place in Leeds at which questions like this come racing into the mind. At the southern boundary, the M1 motorway has arrived from London, destined to fly over the greater part of the city on its way to the true North. A few miles down the carriageway, the M62—the Pennine Motorway—intersects. The architecture of these road systems is spare and economical. It happens to blend well with the landscape round about.

The arrival of the M1 is like that of a harbinger. The old geography of the district, which gives character to disputes with Bradford, disdain of Sheffield, a love and affection for the Dales countryside which is without parallel in Britain, all this has given a history to Leeds. It is a history based on work, on industrial history. The particular character of the work—the way the industry has developed—has modified without entirely destroying the old forms. That development is now at its limit. Everywhere you go in Leeds, you feel that something else is about to happen.

According to White, who published a directory of Leeds in the middle of the last century, the population in 1801 was 53,302. Half a century earlier it was no more than half that. By 1851, when really reliable census figures were available, it had trebled. It trebled again by the end of the century. In other words, Leeds hardly grew; it erupted. White recorded figures for birth, death and marriage for the half year to 30th June, 1852. There were 4,020 births, and 2,791 deaths; 1,150 people were married. In human terms, the city raged into life. Looking back, we would be tempted to say that as a place to live and work in, it ran away with itself. It is only recently that the inevitable consequences of the Industrial Revolution—the first, half-forgotten jubilant revolution—have come to embarrass us. In this country there are over half a million houses which the Government itself acknowledges as being unfit for human habitation. Most of these were built in the great expansionist days of the last century, when labour was drawn into the cities in the way White describes of Leeds. By comparison with some smaller housing authorities and against the relative standards of what constitutes a reasonable and what a

statutory idea of human habitation, Leeds can claim to have
worked hard to minimize the sombre effects of its mushroom
growth. There is still some terrible housing in Leeds (and some
of it quite recent) but there are few conditions quite as stark as
you will find in parts of London or other major provincial cities
which are on the boom. Neither is there evidence of the great
depressions.

This is not to whitewash the place. It is far short of perfection.
In that, it joins the queue with the rest of urban Britain that was
hurried up to meet the contingency of a fantastic opportunity for
work and wealth. But while Leeds has its fair share of physical
ugliness and an unhelpful environment, it has had one great
advantage. As we shall see, although the city was founded on
wool, it has diversified its industries almost as a model of *laissez
faire* economics. By luck or judgement, the growth of industry
ran across the board and protected workers from the stunning of
blows, prolonged unemployment and economic stagnation. There
is a great variety of work in Leeds today, and there has been for
most of this century. This has more than once saved the city.
Other Northern cities have been less lucky. This is true of
Bradford, even, which is so close by. The slump hit Bradford far
harder than its upstart neighbour.

In the first thirty or forty years of the last century, however,
Leeds housing was synonymous with bad housing. In certain
areas, and everywhere among the poorest people, conditions were
appalling. It is almost incredible that Leeds was not a properly
constituted or represented borough until 1832 and then only in
the terms which applied at the time. The Commissioners on
Municipal Corporations, who prepared the way for the Act of
1835, visited Leeds in 1833. They reported the corporation to be
of "absolute and uncontrolled self-election. Family influence is
predominant. Fathers and sons, brothers and brothers-in-law
succeed to the offices of the corporation like matters of family
settlement." It was only a year since Leeds had been able to elect
a Parliamentary representative at all, and the proper reorganization of local government was to take much longer. Not until
after the Municipal Corporation Act of 1835 was there any
statutory provision for water, gas or sewage.

The first Member of Parliament for Leeds was the historian

Macauley. He faced an extraordinary situation. In an uneventful year the death rate was three times what it is today. There was the threat of epidemic disease on a crippling scale—in fact cholera broke out in 1832 and 1848, and typhus in 1847. The city was pulling labour in faster than it could build, and its building was left in the hands of property speculators. The land was freehold, and divided among many dozens of landlords. The tidal pull of work and jobs had practically swept away responsible planning and government.

The people who controlled Leeds in those early days rode a tiger. Young men—Gott, Baines, Barran, Matthew Murray, Broderick—flew to the top. Whole industries were born. Barran is a case in point. In his Leeds factory the ready-made clothing industry leapt up on the freshly minted patent for Singer's sewing machine. At the very outset of the century Gott's Bean Ing Mills had been one of the dozen biggest employers of labour in the whole country, with 1,000 hands, of whom 500 were women and children. Gott himself was a mere lad of thirty. There were fortunes to be made.

Without a liberal conscience of any kind, such a society would have destroyed itself just as Marx predicted, within his lifetime. Leaving conscience to one side, and purly in terms of self-interest and its own protection, the new Victorians were forced to act. Reorganization was crucial. Until 1843, Leeds drank its own sewage. The River Aire received the sewage and supplied the town with water from the same three miles. The place had to become less dangerous before it could become more tolerable. Few of these most hideous scars now remain, yet Leeds is a notable example of a city of great size lacking a substantial physical heart. The erection of the town hall, on a specially mounded site away from the old centre, was an attempt in 1858 to begin a handsome and fitting municipality in the Victorian taste. Such a thing was never completed. The town had reordered its priorities, but the great civic centre which such wealth and prestige deserved never materialized. The loss to Leeds is permanent.

Broderick's town hall is a great landmark. It is a massive, blackened building of great weight and authority literally out on its own. Its grave stare is returned by the squint of a miserable terrace on the other side of the Headrow; but never mind. The town hall has the uncomfortable prestige of being simply big, black and Victorian, but it is not ugly. On the contrary, it has rather a handsome, graceful exterior that was and still is the envy of many another corporation. With his designs for this building, the young Cuthbert Broderick hit the jackpot.

He was born in Hull in 1822 and articled at fourteen to the Bradford architects Lockwood and Mawson. When he was twenty-two, Broderick visited France and Italy, taking his drawing block with him. It was the age of Pugin in English architecture and the advocacy of a return to Gothic models for great churches and public buildings. Pugin himself was a tireless enthusiast of Gothic. His ideas and the shock of discovering for himself the great cathedrals of Caen, Carentan and Rouen made an immediate impression on Broderick. He returned with a full sketch book and great ambitions. When he was offered a partnership in his firm, he refused and set up in his own account. His first commission was for a small and unimportant railway station in his native East Riding.

His chance came in 1852, when he was still only twenty-nine. His design for Leeds Town Hall was ingenious and inventive and managed to suggest that controlled passion which was the special character of the Victorians. His plans had size and grandeur and simplicity (his original elevations were beautifully austere). But in the detail, especially in the interior, there is a feeling of excitement. The interior is a young man's love-affair with wealth and power. Some of it is absurd, some of it beautiful. The whole design found great favour with the corporation. To everybody's amazement, Broderick beat his former employers into second place in the competition for a satisfactory design. A contract was duly let for £41,835. This sum proved to a woeful underestimate, as things like this generally turn out; the completed building cost three times as much and was a munificent endowment by any standards.

There is an interesting story concerning the tower, a curious, bold cupola supported on columns which echo the Corinthian columns of the south façade. In their deliberations of 22nd August 1853, the council found that they felt the want of a good tower, something to top off Broderick's designs. In its original form, the town hall would have presented a very unsentimental, cool image of civic pride. Although the building was erected on an artificial mound, its proportions kept it low and its embellishment was spare. The tower, which of course has no practical function, adds a quality which is almost that of levity. Without it, the building might be considered a little pompous. No doubt the council were after a bit of pomp, and they called for an estimate. The estimated cost was a further £7,500. With characteristic northern caution, of the belt and braces kind, the council ordered £1,500 to be spent on strengthening the walls to receive the tower, pending their further discussion. The tower was finally added in 1856.

Another feature of the present building added after the publication of the original plans was the lions at either side of the steps. During discussion of this idea, Broderick happened to be in Hull, supervising the building of its town hall. He stopped to speak to an exceptionally good mason on the site. "Why man," Broderick exclaimed, "you're a sculptor." "No, sir, nothing but an ordinary carver." Broderick sent this man to Regent's Park Zoo to look at lions and model them from the life. When this tender was invited, it was won by Broderick's new ally.

The building was opened in 1858 by Queen Victoria. The Prince Consort was able to assure the ecstatic architect that Her Majesty found great favour with his work. It was the start of Broderick's brief but adventurous fame. In 1860 he designed the Corn Exchange, Leeds; a very handsome elliptical building that deserved a far better fate. Today it has miserably sunk to a brief way of describing a bus-route terminus: very few people can have gone inside. In the same year as the Corn Exchange, he completed the commission for the old Station Hotel in City Square (now replaced by a particularly unimpressive successor). In 1864, he completed Blenheim Baptist and Headingley Hill Congregational churches. The following year he added the Leeds Institute to the city centre, a heavy, rather tired design that now houses the Civic Theatre, Leeds Music Centre and Jacob Kramer College of Art in pleasant and somehow independent cacophony.

In 1866 Broderick prepared and submitted designs for the National Gallery in London. Had he been successful here, Leeds

would have perhaps honoured him the more. He was not, and
in 1869, aged forty-seven and a rich bachelor, he retired to Paris.
He arrived just in time to be involved, as one of its newest citizens,
in the Siege of Paris, but survived that to paint and potter in
comfort and, one supposes, gentlemanly indolence. Broderick's
talent was an unusual one for the new, responsible Leeds to have
stumbled on. He was a lucky architect in a profession where
mistakes tend to be long-lasting. He hit a particular nail squarely
on the head for Leeds and although his work was in a sense left
uncompleted—for the 'centre' of the city has swung this way and
that ever since—his great monument, the town hall, is very
affectionately regarded. Black as soot, and nothing if not obvious,
it is something to live by in a city centre of more than ordinary
architectural confusion. It is a little ironic that the tower and
cupola which were added with such prudence as an afterthought
are the parts of the design easiest remembered and most often
quoted in sightseers' photographs. The Græco-Roman austerity
of the building proper is much more difficult to appreciate in
prospect: what ever might have happened round about never did.

Victorian Leeds liked big churches and there the Gothic
Revival, in Broderick's two greatest designs, had already had
its head, particularly in the work of Chantrell, who rebuilt
the parish church between 1838 and 1841. The parish church of
Leeds has a miserable architectural history. Chantrell's church was
the fifth on that site, which was very close to the original place
of birth of Leeds as a community of any size at all. (In fact the
architect discovered fragments of the original market cross, which
was a symbol of commercial viability, built into the old church
tower. These he lightly removed to the garden of his house in
Brighton, and it was not until after his death that the parish won
them back again.)

If the town hall is on the periphery of the city proper, the parish
church can be said to be apparently shunted down a side street.
The line of the church, which is richly and ornately Gothic, runs
parallel to a railway embankment on the other side of the road.
In time the city section of the M1 will practically skim its eastern
end. Its bells, which replaced a famous peal in the old church, are
said to be the first ever to travel to a site by railway, an honour
they repaid in tribute at every opening of a new line to Leeds. It

was perhaps an over-enthusiastic acknowledgement of modern times. In a topographical sense, Chantrell's parish church was swiftly ignored by its parishioners. The elusive true centre of the city was elsewhere.

The most decisive stroke in what little overall planning central Leeds has had was in the widening and extension of the Headrow, the west-east 'main street' of the city and this came about as a Draconian measure in the present century, between the wars. We shall need to look at this brutal solution again (especially since it has now been reproduced only a few yards to the north by a massive inner ring road). For the moment we shall do better by looking at the city overall, in an attempt to get some idea of its peculiar atmosphere.

Leeds brick is soft and red. The city is famous and was notorious for its back-to-back houses, in which a party wall runs the length of the street giving two houses in little more than the width of one. It is these back-to-backs, many of them, that are being torn down today. You can still see far too many back-to-backs, with washing strung across the narrow streets from lamp-posts: but great changes are taking place. From any high window in the city centre, the encircling skyline bristles with new tower blocks. In a few years the red city of the Victorian working classes will have disappeared. The most infamous areas have been no more than memories for many years.

What is left of Victorian housing in Leeds is amazingly various. They quarried stone along the banks of the river in the eighteenth century and made it profitable. Stone-built houses, or decorative stone facing, is a sign in Yorkshire of respectability and wealth. To a southern eye the results are often slightly forbidding. These houses are tall and solidly built. Their decorations—plaster-moulded ceilings, tiled halls, stained-glass window lights, speak of a solid, cautious, canny set of people. Around the city centre the ring of what were once proud and independent villages boasts housing of this kind—stiff, highbuttoned, *quiet* groves and avenues and crescents. Beyond this ring and folded round it are the newer suburbs, the semi-detacheds, the parades of shops, the newer schools, the more conspicuous green spaces. Beyond that, and with startling suddenness, is the countryside.

Because the city is formed into loose concentric circles in this fashion, Leeds is a particularly interesting place in which to househunt. Where in London you will find a whole borough formed from identical dwellings, or with a nob hill firmly set aside from encroachment by a particular road or park, in Leeds there is variety and oddity round almost every bend.

Middle-class Leeds built for its purse and for the weather. The air is some degrees colder than in London and the summers are shorter. Gardens are weeks behind the south. A really warm day in summer is a delightful surprise. The squares fill with lunch-hour typists who, however relaxed they look in the sunshine, probably keep a cardigan in the desk-drawer back at the office. It is not the late and short summers that one regrets but the miserable winters. Even the most ardent enthusiast can find little to recommend a winter in Leeds. For weeks on end a dreary cloud seems to settle over the roofs. What would be just a spell of bad weather on a farm is transformed by the congestion of the city into a half-lit misery. When the snow falls, there is not much romance and far too much road-salt about. Since the Smoke Abatement Act things are much better; but before then—and particularly in the great expansionist days—the atmosphere must have been truly Dickensian.

If it is sometimes dirty it is not a gloomy city, however. The land rises and falls as you traverse it, concealing and revealing its vistas unexpectedly. There are some generous and heavily wooded parks—of which more in their place. There are some remarkable areas of a character and atmosphere all their own. Above all, there is a kind of drive and energy on the streets and in the way the traffic moves around that make Leeds seem busy to the point of preoccupation. There are some really terribly city-centre develop-ments and no one (except a Leodensian) would describe Leeds as beautiful, much less gay. But while there are some daunting qualities, gloominess is not one of them. Half a million fairly prosperous, fairly self-confident people live here. For the past ten years the most common sight as they go to work has been the tower crane and the road drill. It is as though there is an energy to replace as fierce as the founding fathers' lust to build.

II

"LOIDIS IN ELMETE"

IN THE very beginning, Leeds was little more than a fording place on the Aire. Holbeck and Sheepscar Beck would flood in winter, recede in summer. The silts they carried down to the main stream built up in time to a maze of banks and shallows across the marshes. Romans had found this path across the broad sluggish valley, which linked so usefully with the limestone uplands where their route of march lay. Although no trace remains, it is clear that a road once existed between the vital garrisons of York and Chester: once Roman fires burned in the damp nights around the present-day Adel. In the Roman occupation of Britain, the Leeds region was the outback, the unvalued and unconsidered hill-forest area that must have displeased many a baggage party and relief column.

In the Dark Ages the region was within a minor British kingdom and may have been the camp headquarters in the squabbles, pillage and outright warfare between the Britons and their Mercian enemies. Elmet was the name of this early kingdom, a name that survives in many a village today. Elmet or Elmete was probably a large area, from the Don to Ripon, with present-day Leeds at its westerly boundaries. The Venerable Bede mentions the *regio* of Loidis, adding a note about the stone altar of an early church "preserved in the monastery that lies in Elmete Wood". Some authorities believe that the parish church of St. Peter's was that monastery, and Elmete Wood a fair description of Leeds as it was about 730. In any political organization centred on the vale that spreads out from the foot of the Pennine Hills, Leeds would be a densely wooded frontier post, and perhaps the last resort of a beleaguered kingdom. As the fierce struggles for Elmete came to their head, the place name came to mean the area around Leeds, no more than that.

28

The complicated history of Yorkshire at this time is a story of struggle between Danes, Norse, English and Britons. In the parish church of Leeds are fragments of religious decorations and symbols that were discovered when Chantrell demolished the old tower. They reveal a complete mingling of influences. The great prizes to be won were to the east and centred round York, yet because of Leeds' strategic relationship to the Aire Gap through the Pennines, it had a vital frontier role to play. But like a frontier town, nothing permanent or solid was laid down. It was not so much the settlement as the region that was important.

We know from the Domesday Book what size the settlement was in 1086. It comprised "Ten caracutes of land, six oxgangs to be taxed and land to six ploughs; seven thanes held it in the time of King Edward for seven manors. Twenty-seven Villanes and four Sokemen and four Bordars have now these fourteen ploughs. There is a priest and a church and a mill of four shillings and ten acres of meadows." The Domesday Book, which was a mammoth inventory and stocktaking of the lands the Conquest had won, also mentions Armley, Beeston, Bramley, Osmanthorpe, Chapel Allerton, Headingley and Hunslet. All these places now fall within the city boundary.

A caracute of land comprised about 100 acres, and an oxgang was the unit of land an ox might plough in one day. Sokemen and Bordars were yeoman farmers, with some independence. The villanes were serfs. The purpose of the Domesday Book was to indicate what could be taxed. As a clearing in the waste lands of Yorkshire, Leeds and its neighbouring villages was clearly taxable. But it would need a considerable imaginative feat to recreate this early Leeds as a powerful or even a noted place in the contemporary pattern. We can guess that the spirit of the place was dour and sullen, in an age when wolves roamed the high ground above Chapel Allerton and the region was better known for its dripping woods than its open spaces. We can look at the condition of the area 100 years after the Conquest by examining a ruin that has been tidied away in the subsequent history of Leeds proper.

Kirkstall Abbey dates from 1152. There is a nice story of the twelve founding monks sheltering under a bush from the winter weather while God and their abbot considered the advantages of the site. They found it a good one, hard by the river on the north bank of the Aire. The river is a glacial cut through the soft rocks surrounding the coal measures and the coarser, tougher millstone grit. At this point in its passage the river ran clean and fast. Beneath Kirkstall the valley broadened and the stream grew wider and more sluggish. The marshes to the east betokened shallower water. Just out of sight downriver was the crossing point which had given rise to the settlement of Leeds.

The monks who settled at Kirkstall were Cistercians, an order which had only come into England thirty years earlier. They were the white monks, whose greatest monument is at Fountains Abbey, thirty miles away on the Skell. While Fountains was being built under the watchful patronage of the Archbishop of York, smaller communities of monks were enticed away by more modest patrons. The de Lacy family endowed one such community. Henry de Lacy, grandson of the great Conqueror baron, lay in fear of death at Pomfret Castle. He vowed to build an abbey if he should recover from his illness. The first de Lacy endowment was at Barnoldswick, then a particularly bleak and deserted spot.

Cistercians were founded from a desire to reintroduce austerity into monastic life. But Abbot Alexander and the twelve monks who struggled with the elements at Barnoldswick were at last forced from their upland miseries to search for a more realistic site. When they prospected the Aire valley at Kirkstall they found the site already occupied by hermits. These recluses had been granted a vision of just such a northern valley as this and travelled from the south to find it. The auspices for a religious foundation could hardly have been better, especially as the hermits agreed to surrender to the Cistercian rule. Their actual standard of living probably improved considerably. When Abbot Alexander discovered them they were eking out a miserable life of piety in makeshift bivouacs constructed from fallen branches.

The abbey church and the conventual buildings were completed within thirty years and Alexander lived to see the dream realized. It is legend that both the abbot and his benefactor, Henry de Lacy, were interred within the abbey. The building was a remarkable achievement, 224 feet long and 62 feet wide across the nave and side aisles. Bearing in mind that the church replaced a few miserable bowers in a dense wood and was the biggest building of any kind the length of the Aire, it was a tribute to more than piety. The building of the abbey was a considerable piece of civil engineering. In the next fifty years after Alexander's death, the abbot's house, infirmary, guest house and chapter house were completed. The community thrived. De Lacy lands were spread all over Yorkshire and the abbey was crucially placed among the ten small townships of Leeds. What it did, Leeds copied. The Cistercians were hard-headed businessmen as well as monks and their method of farming was revolutionary.

J. S. Fletcher was an Edwardian who wrote a three-volume *Picturesque History of Yorkshire*. When he came to visit Kirkstall, the place baffled him. "Probably no religious foundation in England had a less eventful history than that of Kirkstall, and its story serves to show that whatever good purposes some of the conventual establishments served, there were others which appeared to have no real reason for existence."

Fletcher was searching for something to say about an abbey which has the most austere of all monastic architecture. After the Dissolution Kirkstall seems to have sunk into almost complete oblivion. It was pillaged then and the roof and beams stripped out. The tower collapsed into the nave in 1779 and the nave screens which were once a key to the life of the monastery had long since disappeared. As an historic site, Kirkstall seemed to have most appeal to water-colourists and curious visitors to 'Gothic' remains. It was not seriously studied for what it was until 1890, by which time ivy had reclaimed its place and trees had grown in among the stones.

Its rehabilitation in this century embodies a curious irony. Although little is known of the commercial activities of Kirkstall in its heyday, it is a fact that Cistercian monasteries had a trade between each other that was rich and complex. This trade favoured the order in general rather than a local community, or any secular interest. When Alexander started building at Kirkstall there was a little community around the Roman ford. There was there a rudimentary church and a mill. But Leeds did not have a market until 1258 and its annual fair was not granted until 1322. Historians have suggested that even in those days Leeds was a place of work, of industry, first and a place of trade only after.

The abbey effectively strangled the tiny township on the marshes. It is ironic therefore that when St. John Hope took an axe to the mass of ivy and scrub growing throughout the abbey, he repaired the damage time had made. For in time the town had prospered and the abbey had died. The church which had once been the religious centre of so much prosperous trading, as far afield as Burgundy, was now open to the public as an interesting curiosity —although not interesting enough for Fletcher's itching pen.

St. John Hope's clearing operations at the beginning of this century marked the first scholarly attempts at restoration. The site had been plundered heavily for its building materials at the time of the Dissolution. Anything of value, fixed or portable, had been chopped out and carried away. For generations after whenever good cut stone was wanted the abbey provided a ready source. The collapse of the tower in the eighteenth century probably set its seal as a forsaken place. No one came along to landscape it as part of their gardens or dug to search for possible buried treasures. The elements and the land took their revenge on Kirkstall.

An abbey is a curious monument. As it happens, Cistercian monasteries abound in Yorkshire. Without the help of the museum which has been built up within the abbey gatehouse, it is doubtful whether this late restoration would be of any great interest in Leeds. To see a Cistercian foundation in exquisite surroundings in Yorkshire, you go to Fountains, the mother of Kirkstall. There the landscape has been contrived in the eighteenth century to set off the 'awful aspect' of the abbey and tame its Gothic horrors within the elegant pale of an Augustan garden. Kirkstall is a very fine example of Norman architecture but a little defeating to an untrained eye. When it was acquired by the corporation a park was created from the immediate grounds with walks and asphalt paths. Take these away, and you see Kirkstall as it might have been within its walled enclosure in medieval times. It is a further irony of the abbey's life that it perhaps more than any other has remained comparatively free from eighteenth-century interest in medieval barbarities, as they thought of the period then. What we have in Kirkstall is a relic of a workaday monastic life.

We can reconstruct something of the terms of that life from

The ruins of Kirkstall Abbey Church

literary sources. We know for example that Cistercians were vowed much more strictly by their order than by the old Benedictine rule which they tried to supersede. The rigours of the Yorkshire climate made monastic simplicity a phrase with more than mere spiritual meanings. This was at any rate true to begin with. In the earliest days, the sacrist rang for his brothers at two in the morning. They filed down from the dorters into the church for service. A second service was held at break of day and a third when the sun was properly up. When these observances had been completed the brothers adjourned to the chapter house where they received instruction in the form of prayers and criticism. The fourth service was at half-past eleven, after which the monks took their first food of the day in the refectory. This was a hot meal—the only hot meal—of stunning vegetarianism.

As Benedict had observed, "Idleness is an enemy of the soul." During the meal one monk would read aloud to the rest from the lives of the saints. An hour's rest followed. Then the monks took themselves off to their work, joining the lay brotherhood in the fields and barns. The evening meal was of uncooked vegetables and bread and was digested in contemplation and study within the cloisters of the abbey. Evening services concluded a day which was complete by eight o'clock. The physical conditions of that day would have been tiredness, hunger and cold. The whole twenty-four hours was part of a regulation of life that required almost pathological obedience.

Such an intellectual and physical submission is difficult to make, although extremely attractive in certain historical conditions and to a certain personality in any period. We can deduce a little more of the struggle to maintain this rigour from the abbey itself. For example, there are two kitchens. In time, as the order grew older, it admitted meat on certain days only. At first this was rare, then more common in diet, but under such strictness that a separate kitchen was built to house and cook the meat. We can also see the division there was between the literate monks who celebrated Mass (and in the early days anyone who could say a Mass was required to say it, which explains the significance of the side chapels) and the lay brotherhood, who were bound by the same rule but not admitted to the canonical masses.

A stone screen once separated the nave of the church into two.

3

Steps in working-class Meanwood worn down by clogs

The religious community had access from their dorters to the eastern end of the church. On the other side of the screen, the lay brothers were admitted to church. It is likely that a second screen also existed and in the narrow space between the sick and infirm were cared for, or left to languish. The earliest parts of Kirkstall would have been exceptionally dark even in high summer, and religion must have appeared far more of a doubtful, frightening mystery than it now seems to the majority. The scale of the buildings at Kirkstall and the almost superhuman devotions of their builders were a testament in themselves to the fierceness of the intellectual struggle going on inside the walls. Abbeys were not endowed from rich men's purses because rich men had that obligation. They were endowed because rich men were terrified out of their minds. There was nothing poetic or quaintly pleasing about hearing a Mass being chanted at two in the morning. The sounds were a reassurance. The prayer-factory was doing its job.

Kirkstall became in time a trading centre as well as a church. It communicated much more than prayer. The building of a guest house and Abbot's lodgings are an indication of its outward responsibilities and wealth. The gatehouse which houses the museum is a reminder of the wall which once surrounded the estate. The present Kirkstall Road runs within the line of this wall. Behind it, at the time of Chaucer, was a virtual village in its own right, of much greater wealth and influence than Leeds itself.

The trade the monasteries carried on best was wool. They were given the waste lands which were of lesser importance to their secular protectors. They pioneered the uplands. They were both producers of wool and dealers in it. When the fulling mill was brought into England, they became finishers. The Knights Templar developed the watermill—Temple Newsam had such a fulling mill in 1185. Kirkstall did its own fulling, weaving and dyeing. It probably smelted ores as well. It traded within the closed economic community of its brother monasteries. Pieces of French and Italian maiolica have been discovered in excavation. Recent research has shown the importance of Kirkstall as a centre for the manufacture and distribution of pottery.

All this went on despite the Leeds townships and not because of them. We must imagine Kirkstall as having not one but many plumes of smoke rising from within its walls and not a narrow

track but a broad muddy lane to its gates. In the days when
Kirkstall prospered, the great towns of Yorkshire were yet to
exist. Across the heavy woods, riding by outgranges of the
mother-monastery, far from the valley of the Aire, lay York. The
York of the Guilds, the York of the great Minster was the focus
of Yorkshire, not the wild rural parts of the valley-system. The
wealth was in the plains. In this pattern, Kirkstall was important
for its industry and its commerce. Men would know of
Kirkstall and its borrowings on next year's yield who had
never turned their horse's head into the quiet lane that led to
Leeds.

Dissolution of the monasteries loosened the stranglehold on the
township. We can go back to the early days to see a little of the
growth of life there. In 1207 the de Lacy family granted Maurice
Paganel a charter for the town, which had the effect of allowing
the people to pay rent rather than service. Paganel or Paynel was
descended from a Norman lord, but perhaps one forced to run for
his money. We know at any rate that when Maurice was captured
in the battle of Lincoln, which was a battle against King John, he
pledged the manor of Leeds against his ransom and never
recovered it. The manor of Leeds was a parcel of Norman lands
many times mentioned in laborious documents passed this way
and that in council. It was part of a larger struggle for power in
the North of England in which the de Lacy family was seldom
far from the centre. Pontefract, where the first de Lacy had set his
palatial castle, was the powerhouse. The charter granted to Leeds
enabled at least some of its tenants to buy and sell land, deal in
goods, run their own justice, and move the goods they made or
bought "by water and by land, whithersoever they will, without
impediment and without paying custom, unless they are forbidden
to do so by the lord or his bailiffs".

In other words, this first charter permitted the burgesses of Leeds
to get on with it, although only within the terms of the Norman
Conquest. The lord of the manor was a distant, absent landlord—
for example from 1361 to 1399 the lord was Shakespeare's John
of Gaunt, who as well as being Duke of Lancaster was also feudal
King of Castile and Leon, Duke of Aquitane, and Lord of
Bergerac. The resonance of these titles, if it carried at all to Leeds,
could have had little practical significance to the men who were

pushing back the forest, clearing the millstreams, planting grain and building in boulder stone the farms and houses of the manor. When old John of Gaunt's son, Henry Bolingbroke, seized the crown (while the king languished in Pontefract Castle), the manor of Leeds became a royal manor.

Its chief riches were its waters. Fulling is one of the final processes in the making of cloth. York and Beverley had for generations tried to keep the production of cloth within their power, but the invention of the fulling mill was in a way the very first industrial process to revolutionize the Aire and Calder valleys. We can see how the exchange in power between the monastic order and the town took place peaceably from the fate of the last Abbot of Kirkstall. Well over 200 monastic institutions were affected by the Dissolution in Yorkshire alone. Their collapse had been foreshadowed internally. When the time came, the abbot had little expectation of being hounded to death, but rather more of being accommodated. So he was. He was pensioned at £66 a year and converted the abbey gatehouse into his private residence. He lived there until his death in 1568.

The trade in wool had changed Leeds from a few crude clearings to "a praty market having one Paroche Church, reasonably well buildid, and a as large as Bradeford but not so quik as it". So Leland described Leeds at about the time that John Ripley converted the abbey gatehouse. There were seven fulling mills turning in the town, a stone chantry-bridge across the Aire. The great Elizabethan expansion was about to take place.

The grammar school dates from 1552, and the Moot Hall from 1561. These are the signs of growth. At the time of the building, in 1376, of the first Leeds bridge or at any rate the first substantial bridge in stone (it lasted well into the eighteenth century), Leeds was second in population to Wakefield. But in Shakespeare's time Leeds overtook its ancient rivals, Wakefield and Pontefract. In the next 100 years, Leeds grew to be three times as large as Wakefield, measured in terms of the numbers of houses. The Elizabethan Age which Shakespeare and Spenser celebrated with such affection seems to have kissed remote Leeds with some of its magic. It is in this period that we can begin to sense some of the sterling qualities Leeds today prizes so highly. Nicholas Raynton provides a description of the place as it was in 1628:

Leeds hath a large and broad streete—paved with stone—leading
directlie north and continuallie ascendinge. The houses on both
sides thereof are verie thicke and close compacted together, being
ancient meane and low built; and generally all of Tymber ... only
some fewe of the richer sort of the Inhabitants have theire houses
more large and capacious, yett all lowe and straightened on their
backsides. In the middle of the streete (towards the upper end wheare
the Markett place standeth) is built the Court or Moote House. ...

This description fits Leeds at the time of its royal charter of
incorporation as a borough, which dates from 1626. The granting
of the charter can be seen as the fulfilment of vigorous trading and
the rise to power of a group of merchants determined to press
home the advantages of being "from henceforth and forever a
free borough of itself" and that "the saide borough of Leeds and
the circuit, jurisdiction and precinct thereof from henceforth for
ever may be and shall extend and stretch into and throughout the
whole town and parish of Leeds aforesaid". By the enactment of
this charter, the Crown assured Leeds a place as the most important
market town in the West Riding. Two years after it was sealed,
the old Manor of Leeds, with all its fusty titles, was bought back
from Charles I, who was searching for ways to pay off his father's
debts.

When Kirkstall fell (and as it languished into old age) Leeds
rose. The purchase of the manor, so casually negotiated by
Richard Sykes, one of the new breed of merchants, ended the old
confusion of loyalties and dues, the old constrictions and checks
on free growth. Old manorial lands became freehold, old taxes
fell in disuse, the bailiffs lost their powers. The purpose of the
charter was to secure a monopoly and protect a trade and make its
burgesses rich. In 1661, after the Restoration, a new borough
charter was granted (decorated with a pen-and-ink drawing of
the new monarch) which gave the town its first mayor and its
first full aldermanic benches. The sudden sturdiness Leeds seems
to have acquired in Elizabethan times was now confirmed in all
constitutional dignity. Thomas Danby, mayor, walking with
George Bannister, his town clerk, could reflect with something
recognizably modern in feeling on the measure and purpose to be
found in their town. 'Northern Dozens' as the local cloth was
known throughout the kingdom, were being woven in a dozen

and more places within a few minutes' walk of the Moot Hall. The fulling mills were spinning energetically and the tenters' fields (from which the expression 'on tenterhooks') were spread with cloth.

The forgotten idyll that was ushered in at this time is enticingly fugitive. Walking round present-day Leeds you can sometimes see its ghost flit. On a late summer evening in Leeds, when all the wheels have stopped turning, and the light is falling from the sky, you can sometimes feel the quiet satisfaction that must have stood in the fields which are now streets. In the eighteenth century, Leeds was no small hamlet, but a town of some 17,000. Since its incorporation it has hardly ever known poverty. It was about three times the size of Oxford, as Oxford then was. We would not consider it anything very special today, if we were by some time-fluke landed back in it; but we might have been surprised by its confident bearing, dignity and calm. There were many larger market towns in the country and many with more elegance and style about them than Leeds. Yet what had been made from a Norman manor about the size of ten football pitches was comely in a homespun way. Like its cloth, Leeds was well made and serviceable.

III

THE POT BOILS

IN THE later years of the eighteenth century, before the pot began to boil, Leeds had the time and energy to acquire at least some of the leisurely grace that flowed from the capital. The old Leeds, centred round Briggate, had its own small share of the calm and discipline that many towns and cities in England can still show at their centres. Although a long way from London and traditionally of an independent nature, the West Riding was an immensely rich and aristocratic land. Landed wealth was permanent wealth and had enormous political significance. Yorkshire abounds in fine houses whose foundations were laid in this period. Their architectural style and the style of life they called for in their owners springs from the ample occasion the county aristocracy had to visit London, take its papers, its books, its fashionable ideas. In their way, too, the new wealthy of the clothing districts were eager to learn and to emulate.

A fair indication of this kind of enthusiasm was the opening of the Theatre Royal built in Hunslet Lane, towards the end of the century. Hunslet Lane is the natural continuation of Briggate on the south side of the river. In the eighteenth century it was an area which had aspirations to quality, which the building of the theatre shows. The Royal's actor-manager was one Tate Wilkinson, a clergyman's son from London. His theatre was an immediate success, and, as the first properly licensed theatre in Leeds, drew audiences away from the 'concert rooms' where dramatics had to be mixed with musical entertainment, in order not to infringe the law.

It was soon said of the Leeds stage "it can boast of being the nursery for that of London". Kemble, Macready, Keans and the incomparable Mrs. Siddons played the Royal. Wilkinson was good—or perhaps lucky—with women. His actresses included

Mrs. Jordan, who was the mistress of the Duke of Clarence, afterwards William IV, and was discarded by him later; Elizabeth Farren, who married the twelfth Earl of Derby, and Perdita Robinson who alas was one of the many women who did not marry the Prince of Wales, although she aroused his warm interest. (Caroline of Brunswick was George III's choice of wife for his son: when they first met, the Prince is supposed to have said to a bystander, "I am not well; get me a glass of brandy.")

Wilkinson's repertoire was hectic and uneven, but included the best of every London season. Garrick and Sheridan had given to the theatre a special place in the London scene, as Kemble found when he became stage-manager at Drury Lane. Seldom before or since has the theatre managed to achieve such a peculiar vitality, nor such a widely based audience. In those days it snowed broadsheets and pamphlets whenever a production of Sheridan's irritated his political rivals. The slashing pen of a Gillray was at the ready for the least provocation; the humour was aristocratic and urbane. When the Bishop of Durham said in the House of Lords that the French clearly had a plan for the moral degradation of the country, and was not the practice of lewd dancing at operas just such an instance? the next night's performance of the ballet *Bacchus and Ariadne* was mysteriously postponed. Gillray and his imitators leapt in with a series of caricatures, including the immortally titled "Durham mustard too powerful for the Italian capers".

Although such splendid uproar is not recorded for the Theatre Royal, Hunslet Lane, Wilkinson's theatre was immensely popular and its success is a fair index of public confidence and aspiration, to be set alongside the more sober enterprises of a subscription library, learned societies and the like.

Wilkinson toured his players on a circuit that included Wakefield, Pontefract, Doncaster and, most significantly, York. The Royal at York is still standing and is a flourishing repertory theatre. For York already had an effortless acceptance into the true eighteenth-century community, as any brief stroll through its streets will show. York speaks in full of that 'peace of the Augustans' that Saintsbury described so lovingly. A Roman headquarters, a great walled city of medieval times, a cathedral city whose Minster is one of the finest examples of Gothic in

Yorkshire—there is in York's make-up a quality Leeds never owned nor could. The place has class. It was and is the aristocratic capital of Yorkshire.

At the time when the architect Carr and the cabinet-maker Chippendale of Otley were busy in Yorkshire, making and decorating great houses of stunning casualness, Leeds was in the management of smaller men—the Bischoffs, the Halls and Marshalls. These men were not without their own lineage, but they were simpler, more homespun characters. In their place, and in their time, they were influential and responsible citizens. They *were* citizens. Leeds was their town.

The Hall family, for example, were originally descended from county squires. Theirs was the manor of Stumperlow. They dissipated its wealth in the seventeenth century and recovered their money in all sobriety in Leeds. From 1716 until 1859 the Hall family took office of one kind or another in the town and later on the city. The father, the son, and the grandson were all mayors; the great grandson was returned as Member in 1857— he died the same year. They were loyal, unswerving Whig through thick and thin. In their way, they were to be respected. They saw great changes rock the place to its foundations, but saw little wrong in the worst consequences, and had nothing but pride in the scale of change. They managed as best they could with the tools they had for the job; and it did not cross their mind too often that a Parliamentary system which returned only two members for the whole of Yorkshire—and those members the nominees of the landed interest—was in any way bad for a community which had next to nothing in common with the land.

Henry Clarkson, who lived all his life in Wakefield and was of just such a family as the Halls of Leeds, has left an interesting account of the snap election of 1807, at which his father voted. The only polling booth for the whole county was at York and those who were entitled to vote were carried there at the expense of the candidates. Three candidates contested the 1807 election in search of a majority from only 33,000 votes cast. The expenses of the prospective members were said to be £100,000 each—in fact Henry Lascelles, the son of the Earl of Harewood and the losing candidate, kept a card with that figure on it in his pocket, and produced it in ominous silence whenever asked to stand again. Clarkson was eighty-six in 1887, when he wrote all this down, and its real significance escaped him. It is as though for him the stars of his life were the nobility and gentry of his youth and early manhood, even through the smoke and smother of a momentous century.

Men like that, with that unqualified respect, might have continued in Leeds, had the pressures of industrialization and the growth in population not been truly revolutionary. Indeed, for a time they tried. A Henry Hall was alderman when Brougham's Commissioners into Municipal Corporations arrived in 1832. We have already seen what they had to say. When Macauley resigned his seat in Leeds to go to India, the Hall candidate was Sir John Beckett. Speaking of the commissioner's impending report, he said simply, "I believe the only information that will be conveyed by the commissioner who came into the town of Leeds . . . will be that he found the corporation of Leeds as pure as holy water." Considering the quality of the water in the glass that stood at his elbow, it was a daring metaphor. The sentiments Sir John expressed did not win him the election, but they were extremely popular. Leeds pride saw to that.

As Asa Briggs has pointed out in his book *Victorian Cities*, the Industrial Revolution was a revolution of social structures: nothing like as wholesale as the Luddites and Chartists might have wanted, but nevertheless thoroughgoing and permanent. The reorganization of the old population—or to begin with, its total disorganization—threw up new talents, new leaders, a more divisive difference of opinion. Quite simply, it created a new order. Professor Briggs quotes George Eliot as she came by train to Leeds on the route you yourself have taken at the beginning of this book. She said to her diary: "It is difficult to keep one's faith in a millennium within sight of this modern civilization."

She was passing Hunslet Lane. Smoke and soot had driven out the respectable people who had once walked down pavements noted for their wideness to where Tate Wilkinson had his company of distinguished beauties. The theatre, the solid sheet of town houses, the promise of peaceful, gradual development had all been swept away.

We must go back to the early years of the nineteenth century

again. There they are, walking or riding to the old parish church,
in a town with something of the character of present-day Ripon.
Not exactly a market town, but not too unlike it either. The
adjective English people love best, applied to them, is the word
sturdy. In Yorkshire 'sturdy independence' are words that go
together like bacon and eggs. In this picture of Leeds, the idea
is not very far from the truth.

Dr. Johnson had observed with pleasure that "an English
merchant is a new species of gentleman". From the ranks of the
merchants in a town like Leeds came the magistrates, the vestry
commissioners, the commanders of the militia, the governors of
all local affairs, in fact. They gave the work and to a large extent
they gave the pleasures. When the crowds flocked to Woodhouse
Moor to witness a balloon ascent, or a tattoo, it was under the
genial patronage of the merchants and their families. From the
Leeds Intelligencer of 1792:

> On Monday Last, in consequence of the requisition published in our
> last week's paper, there was the greatest meeting of the Gentlemen,
> Clergy, Merchants and others ever assembled in this borough. The
> Moot-Hall being found incapable of holding them, the Mayor
> adjourned the meeting to the choir of the Parish Church. Upwards of
> four thousand persons were present, who unanimously testified their
> attachment to the King and Constitution of this country by adopting
> the declaration of the Bankers &c of London. . . . Before the meeting
> broke up "God Save the King" was sung twice, in most excellent
> time, accompanied by the organ. The meeting was then dissolved
> and the town's band of music accompanied the Mayor and several
> other gentlemen, who repeated God Save the King at the Market
> Cross and several other places. The effigy of TOM PAINE (properly
> labelled and holding a pair of stays in one hand and his Rights of Man
> in the other) was carried through the principal streets in the after-
> noon, having a halter round his neck, and severely whipped by a
> cartman who followed. In the evening he was hanged at the Market
> Cross, and afterwards thrown into a large bonfire, amidst the shouts
> of the surrounding multitudes.

The merchant was a powerful figure and a paternalistic one.
He was a father to the town in a very practical sense. Parliament
concerned itself very little with schemes of education or welfare,
for example. A good merchant was more than a skilful trader,

he was a figure of authority in a world which took very little account of the majority of the English population.

This is an important point. English local government was literally overwhelmed by the events of the Industrial Revolution. It just could not cope. It was as though the country had set out for a sail on a peaceful river and before knowing it been swept out into the most turbulent of estuaries. We can see something of this indifference to danger when we look at the lack of any plan for national education. In most European countries in the same period, practical schemes of education for the whole population had been advanced and put into practice. In France, in Prussia, in Switzerland and Austria, education was a serious and practical concern of the state. In England the education of the mass of the people was left—by choice—entirely in the hands of the charity schools and Sunday schools. 'Let it alone' was a political philosophy.

In the year of the snap election that Henry Clarkson has described, there was a Bill introduced in Parliament for the general provision of elementary schools. It was tossed out by the Lords. The chief opponents of the Bill were the Lord Chancellor and the Archbishop of Canterbury. The Archbishop's objection was simple enough: that the Bill placed education outside the control of the church. But the Lord Chancellor's objection was stoutly secular. It was Lord Eldon's belief concerning education that too much of it in the wrong hands would lead to laziness, unhappiness and dissatisfaction with the world as it was. (The pub that is closest to the university in present-day Leeds—in fact, bang opposite—is 'The Eldon'.)

As a consequence of these opinions, which took a long time to die, generations of men and women crowding into Leeds and the towns like it, grew up with rather less education and fittedness for life than if they had been born in an open ditch and raised among cattle.

It was for this reason among many others that Victorians were led to exclaim that the poor are always with us. The poor were understood in English law to be more like displaced persons than anything else. The earliest Act of Parliament to deal with them was passed in 1388 and was one of the most expedient pieces of legislation ever. It simply forbade a man to be a vagrant and without work. If someone was unfortunate enough to be without work at the passing of the Act, he was to stay where he was. He was then sent back to his birthplace. If that did no great good, he was whipped. For a second offence he lost his ears. The third time up, he was hanged.

It will come as no surprise to learn that this early Act was not without its shortcomings. People do not choose to be without work and starving and they will not go away when they are told to. In 1601 an Act was passed which was the basis of the Poor Law provisions for over 200 years. Under this Act the church-warden of the parish and two, three or four nominated house-holders should become overseers of the poor. Their duty was to maintain the poor out of local taxation and set them to work. The workhouse became a part of English social life. As a beckoning disaster for the poor, its effect was deep and wounding. Dickens did not draw attention to the workhouse system in *Oliver Twist*. He played fiercely on a nerve that had been exposed in the poor for two centuries. Neither did the fear decrease after Dickens had spoken his mind. Anyone of working-class background who can remember his grandparents will know of the terror the word itself could strike.

We have some figures to show the extent of the Poor Law provisions. In 1776 the cost was £1,530,800. By 1817 it had increased to £7,870,801. Part of this soaring cost was the product of a decision taken by the magistrates of Speenhamland, in Berkshire. Meeting in May 1795, they decided against fixing a minimum wage, which by ancient law they had the right to do. Instead, they brought up the earnings of the poorest workers from supplementary benefits from the rates. The intention may have been good but the results were disastrous. The employers no longer had to pay a living wage, the worker had to apply to the poor rates, and the ratepayer had it forced down his throat the whole time that he was subsidizing what he soon learned to call idleness and imprudence. It was a recipe for a hard, unfeeling, unforgiving relationship between master and man.

When the good people of Leeds burned the effigy of Tom Paine it was in an excess of patriotic zeal. Paine's ideas included maternity benefits and free and universal education. Some of the hatred felt for Paine arose from hatred of these principles. The merchants of Leeds, like their counterparts up and down the country believed in encouraging prudence and industry—in other words the virtues they knew best from their own class. They were root and branch opposed to anything that encouraged the mass of the people to idleness. A man that was starving was a man who had not tried hard enough. One might make an exception for the disabled or the old or the orphaned: but was not the basis of all life work? Work, work, and more work. The wheels were beginning to turn faster and faster. The smoke that had begun to blow across the old town was a sign of the industry of its people.

Nothing captures the Leeds character more than the sudden, volcanic awakening that came in these early years of the last century. There was work to be had in the town. There was great work to be done and the more that was accomplished, the more work it created. It was a completely new version of work and threw up appalling new problems. But once the wheels began to turn, the work itself became an absorption. Where the town had been walking, it was running. Where it had been talking, it was shouting. In 1815, we see from the map of the town that green fields were a five-minute walk in any direction. Park Square was laid out, but on the other side of the road, where the town hall is now, stood a farm. The hunt hounds occasionally broke loose in the streets and kept the good citizens awake in their beds.

A child born in 1815, if he was lucky enough to live forty years, would see some vast changes, nearly all of them arising from the work done in Leeds. The needs of the population were described by the work they did. Like a blind worm, the remorseless effort threw up new tracts of housing to the north and east of Leeds. In the very worst of these, houses were built upon existing ditches. A ditch gave the opportunity for cheap cellars. Into the cellars went the work-people. The new phenomenon of these houses and these streets was their feelings of density. The world for many of those who would live and die in Leeds was simplified to a mass of people, living very close together. A thick, smoky, noisy, dangerous environment grew from the relics of the old town. There were parts of Leeds that were never visited by the well-to-do and respectable. A life was made, came into the world and guttered. The one constant in that life was the need to work.

In Leeds, for far too long, that meant the work of children themselves. The labour of children in Leeds helped to build it.

Leeds is short on public statues. The greatest monument to the city is unrecorded in stone, but laid out in bricks and tiles. From the red city that sprang up, the labour of men, women and their children developed the industry, laid the foundations of the present, wrecked and then rebuilt the past. If a visitor finds the local character hard and unrelenting, he must look to something in the history of the place that has gone without monument. They worked in Leeds in order not to starve, and for a great many years they starved to work. Many more were born than survived and those that survived lived short, brutalized lives. The twin wonders they bequeathed to the present generation were that they worked so hard, and retained so much of their self-respect. Their kind of history was hard indeed.

IV

STEAM IMPROVEMENTS

Soon shall thy arm, Unconquer'd Steam! afar
Drag the slow barge, or drive the rapid car;
Or on widewaving wings expanded bear
The flying-chariot through the fields of air.

So, IN 1792, wrote Erasmus Darwin, a pleasant eccentric old
gentleman with an uncanny eye for realities. The technology of
steam certainly transformed England, nowhere faster than in
Leeds. Watts' pioneering patent on a rotative-action steam engine
suddenly rendered the advantages of a water-source less
important. His patent was dated 1782, ten years before Darwin's
poem. We have seen how fast the young men of the 1820s and
'30s seized on the possibilities of steam power. Only sixty years
after Watts took out his patent, Messrs. Benjamin Hicks, Lancashire engineers, were invited to supply the new engine for
Marshall's Flax Mill.

Marshall's New Mills, which were settled in Water Lane after
a false start in Adel, so stimulated the production of flax that in
time Yorkshire accounted for 60 per cent of all the flax-spinning
in the kingdom. Hicks approached the problem of engine building
with something like reverence for a princely house from a humble
tradesman. Size was the thing. The Bolton firm designed an
engine that developed 240 horse-power. The flywheel was 27 feet
high and the slide-valve cylinders were 5 feet deep. The great
beast of an engine turned its colossal flywheel at only nineteen
revolutions per minute. Lucky the man with some flax waste in
his hand, walking round this awesome machine, feeding power
to the whole mill by an underfloor shaft.

For Benjamin Hicks and John Marshall, the staid authority of
that engine, destroyed in 1886 when the whole business was

The entrance to the Leeds–Liverpool Canal, behind City Station

transferred to New Jersey, must have been a satisfying thing. Landed wealth might be all very well, but who had previously changed the face of work in such a revolutionary way? The steady chunk-chunk of that engine was something no man need be ashamed of, something worthy in its own right. The manufacturer, without any of the advantages of birth, inheritance, or even place of business, was fast becoming a person to be feared. If the century was going to be confrontation of progress with feudalism, the manufacturer was there in the vanguard.

The factory system was much more than a new method of production. As we have already seen, it was a system with profound social and political consequences. In Leeds, as throughout the North wherever the chimneys were smoking, the factory was both creating and destroying, building new hopes and crushing old ideals. What Dr. Johnson meant by a new species of English gentleman can be guessed at from his own acquaintance—men of business who practised philanthropy, were curious scholars, loved learning, were patrons of the arts, in short all the things traditionally reserved for the lord in his lofty hall. Eighteenth century Leeds had a small experience of what Johnson meant—as we shall see, the Leeds Library is an example of what goodhearted burghers could do in that direction. Johnson did not live to see the rise of the manufacturing industries and perhaps would not have liked what actually happened.

For it quickly turned out that the handiest form of labour was the labour of young children. Women and young children were not especially cheap labour, but they were the best labour. In Gott's Bean Ing Mills, which were the wonder of Yorkshire and among the biggest employers in the country, half the labour force—500 people—were women and children. It is almost as though small human beings and nimble fingers at the ends of tiny hands were necessary; if necessary, freely available; and if available, eager to be employed.

"The manufacturer considers the human beings who crowd his mill, from five o'clock in the morning to seven o'clock in the evening, but as so many accessories to his machinery, destined to produce a certain and well-known quantity of work, at the lowest possible outlay of capital. To him their passions, habits, or crimes, are as little interesting as if they bore no relation to the

4

High-rise offices over former glories

errors of a system, of which he was a member and supporter."
So wrote Peter Gaskell, a doctor who moved about the cotton
mills of Stockport about the time of the first Factory Commissions. The Parliamentary Committee investigating conditions in
factories was chaired by Sadler, a former merchant of Leeds such
as Johnson intended by his compliment. Michael Thomas Sadler
was a frail, good-natured man whose Select Committee was all
that he had been able to salvage from an attempt to introduce
legislation governing what went on within the new factories.
Self-contained, self-governing, outside the scope of any government legislation, the factories had never before been investigated
by independently constituted enquiries. The appalling conditions
in cotton mills had been known and some weak legislation passed.
But in 1832 the first full nature of the factory system generally
began to be made clear. The very worst aspect of this system was
shown to be the employment of children.

Child labour was of two kinds, apprentice labour and what was
called free-labour. Apprentices were the children of the Poor
Law, otherwise to languish in workhouses. In 1767 Joseph
Hanway, the man who gave England the umbrella as a badge of
rank, forced through Parliament an Act which forced the parish
authorities of London to board out the children in their care at
not less than 2s. 6d. a week. Hanway saved the lives of the children
concerned, for it has been estimated that burials of such pauper
children fell by 2,100 a year. It quickly occurred to parishes that
a good place to board out these children was in the new manufacturing districts. At the age of seven, the children were bound
in apprenticeship to millowners until the age of twenty-one.
Prentice-houses were built against the wall of the mills, and the
children spent their brief lives between these two buildings. In
the hands of a good millowner, they worked no more than
seventy-two hours a week. In the hands of a bad master, they
worked until they dropped. When their apprenticeship was at an
end, they were qualified to do no more than they had done all
their lives.

Free-labour children were those who lived at home with their
parents, whose labour was freely given. The apprentice system
was ended in 1815. In 1811 an enquiry had been set on foot to
find out the fate of 2,000 apprentice-children. Eighty were found

to be dead, 166 "quitted their service, chiefly run away", and 433
were "not satisfactorily or intelligibly accounted for by the
persons to whom they were bound, or by the overseers where
the masters have become bankrupt". Only 750 of the total were
actually in the mills, and working. But although the system of
indenture had ended, the labour of children had been given forty
years of life in England. There is the legendary remark made by
Pitt, when the cotton manufacturers came to him to say that
because of high wages they were unable to meet their taxes. He is
supposed to have replied, "Take the children." In the battle in
Leeds between the old domestic system and the new factories,
children were forced to work whether they were apprenticed or
not. Their labour was spoken of as free, but an out-of-work
weaver who had children of an age to work was refused poor
relief. A child was a wage earner and the mills were hungry for
his labour.

The work the children did most was 'piecing'. Fielden, the
great reformer, once measured the miles walked in piecing in a
twelve-hour shift, work which the defenders of the factory system
described as light work. In his own factory, children walked
twenty miles a day. Samuel Coulson was a tailor from Stanningley
near Leeds. He gave evidence to the Select Committee chaired
by Sadler in 1832. Coulson had three daughters who had gone to
work in a Leeds mill when they were twelve, eleven and eight
years old.

At what time in the morning, in the brisk time, did those girls go
the mills?—In the brisk time, for about six weeks, they have gone at
3 o'clock in the morning, and ended at 10, or nearly half-past at night.

What sort of mills were those?—The worsted mills.

What intervals were allowed for rest or refreshment during those
nineteen hours of labour?—Breakfast a quarter of an hour, and dinner half an hour, and drinking a quarter of an hour.

Is that all?—Yes.

Was any of that time taken up in cleaning the machinery?—They
generally had to do what they call dry down; sometimes this took
the whole of the time at breakfast or drinking, and they were to get
their dinner or breakfast as they could; if not, it was brought home.

Had you not great difficulty in awakening your children to this
excessive labour?—Yes, in the early time we had to take them up
asleep and shake them, when we got them on the floor to dress them,

before we could get them off to their work; but not so in the common hours.

What was the length of time they could be in bed during those long hours?—It was near 11 o'clock before we could get them into bed after getting a little victuals, and then at morning my mistress used to stop up all night, for fear that we could not get them ready in time; sometimes we have gone to bed, and one of us generally awoke.

What time did you get them up in the morning?—In general me or my mistress got up at 2 o'clock to dress them.

So they had not above four hours sleep at this time?—No, they had not.

For how long together was it?—About six weeks it held; it was only done when the throng was very much on; it was not often that.

The common hours of labour were from 6 in the morning till half-past eight at night?—Yes.

With the same intervals for food?—Yes, just the same.

Were the children excessively fatigued by this labour?—Many times; we have cried often when we have given them the little vic-tualling we had to give them; we had to shake them, and they have fallen asleep with the victuals in their mouths many a time.

To this evidence, and to the other materials gathered by Sadler, the short answer of the manufacturers was "Rubbish". Sadler was despised as a sentimentalist; he lost his seat in the first reformed Parliament. Children by now were so completely inte-grated into the economy that the regulation of their hours would affect the hours worked by grown men. Foreign competition was a favourite bogy raised in Manchester, where the best and worst arguments were constantly on everyone's lips. As a decided advantage of the system, it was pointed out, without any irony, that the children of the factories were being taught a quick-wittedness and aptness for life they could never have got at plough, or in the crude cottages of their grandparents. When Sadler stood for Leeds, immediately after the Select Committee, he was vilified on the hustings by Marshall and the historian Macaulay, and failed to get back into Parliament. Two years later he was dead.

When Sadler lost his seat in Parliament, the reformers were without a champion. Led by Parson Bull of Bradford, they went to the Commons and asked the sitting M.P. for Dorset for his help. Anthony Ashley Cooper was then a man of thirty-one, a shy, introverted, deeply religious man. He had read a few accounts of Sadler's work in *The Times*, which was sympathetic to the plight of children, but he had no first-hand knowledge of the Select Committee, had never visited the North of England and was, in his own words, terrified of the whole question. It was this man that the factory reformers tried to persuade to champion their cause.

What Ashley was being asked to do was to promote in Parliament a Bill limiting the hours worked by children to no more than ten a day. When he accepted, he gave away fifteen years of his life, for it was not until that time had passed that he could advise the operatives that the Ten Hours Bill had become law. The story of its vicissitudes in Parliament is a graphic illustration of the courage of Ashley and the stupidity of his opponents. His last and worst opponent was the leader of his own Party, Robert Peel.

The agitation for Ten Hours is a Leeds and Yorkshire story as well as a great Parliamentary struggle by one the greatest philanthropists the nineteenth century was to produce. It had all the makings of a great epic of England—the austere, aloof aristocrat born to wealth and privilege, joining at any rate temporary hands with the mass of men crowded into the new towns, Leeds among them. When Ashley was twenty-five, he confided to his diary: "I fancy myself in wealth and power, exerting my influences for the ends that I sought for it, for the increase of religion and true happiness." It was this man who set out to help Samuel Coulson's little girls and the thousands like them. Although Ashley in time visited the North often, he was always uneasy in the presence of the men, women and children whose lives he had in his hands. On their side, these simple people considered him a saint, and never failed in their loyalty. The Earl of Shaftesbury, as he became, is part of working-class reference even today.

In the Leeds region, Ashley had a vociferous supporter in Richard Oastler. Oastler was ten years older than his Parliamentary hero and as different as chalk from cheese. A Methodist turned 'Church and King Tory', Oastler was one of those physically large men who discover in themselves a talent and pursue it unrelentingly. In time Oastler was known all over Yorkshire for his blunt, blustering, vigorous style. The factory hands dubbed him 'The Factory King'.

In 1830, Oastler attended a meeting at the Cloth-Hall Yard in Leeds, where an address was given by the Rev. R. W. Hamilton. Hamilton said in all piety that the idea of slavery was abhorrent to the English constitution—meaning of course the slavery of negroes, such as Wilberforce, who was the sitting M.P. for Yorkshire, had pledged to remove. A week later, the *Leeds Mercury* received a long and vehement letter from 'A Briton', headed "YORKSHIRE SLAVERY". Oastler took as his target Bradford, but he might as well have chosen Leeds or Huddersfield, where he then lived. The language of his letter is excited and indignant and it created a furore: "The very streets which receive the droppings of an 'Anti-Slavery Society' are every morning wet by tears of innocent victims at the accursed shrine of avarice, who are compelled (not by the cart-whip of the negro slave-driver) but by the dread of the equally appalling thong or strap of the overlooker, to hasten, half-dressed, but not half-fed, to those magazines of British infantile slavery—the worsted mills in the town and neighbourhood of Bradford!!!"

The *Mercury* published Oastler's letter on 16th October. On the 20th the *Intelligencer* published another long letter, which the *Patriot* reprinted two days later. In this letter, Oastler really let go. "Yes, yes! bring all these facts before the public, and show the hideous monster in his native glare. Then ask, shall he go on to conquer, until the manufacture of the empire is concentrated under one large roof, and the world is supplied by one gigantic firm? Till human nature is almost physically and morally destroyed, and all the inhabitants of this land shall be the slaves of one great manufacturing nabob."

Oastler called for Ten Hours a Day and a Time Book Bill, simplified by him to the blanket roar, "No Yorkshire Slavery!" Ten Hour Committees were already in existence and their numbers proliferated. It is really these that we should attend to, for in them the conscience of the middle men—the doctors, lawyers, agents and skilled workers—joins with the helpless cry of the victims of the system. No Oastler could budge a great millowner, nor no Sadler, with his sentimental poems about the last hours of a factory girl. It was almost beyond the powers of

Ashley, far away in Westminster. The agitation for Ten Hours was not carried through by one man or a few men, but by the sheer weight of thousands, formed into committees. When Chartism failed, Ten Hours was an issue even more seriously taken up. We do not know when Samuel Coulson died, nor what become of his three daughters, but it was men and women like these who formed the backbone of opposition. When Ashley first visited Leeds, he was amazed at the decency and restraint that greeted him. "What a sin it is to be ignorant of the sterling value and merit of these poor men. A few words of kindness with them are as effectual as a force of fifty thousand soldiers on a French population."

There had not been as great a violence in Leeds as elsewhere. The Luddites had been active in other parts of Yorkshire, notably Huddersfield. The object of their attention was the hated gig-mill which threw men out of work. In Leeds a mill was destroyed by fire, cloth cut to ribbons and shears broken, all in the early spring of 1812. But in April 100 men attacked the mill belonging to Mr. Cartwright, called Rawfolds, in Liversedge. Cartwright was ready with nine armed men and beat off the attack, killing two of the attackers. The organizers of the raid turned their attention to another merchant, William Horsfall of Ottiwell. On 28th April, on his way home to Marsden, Horsfall was shot by a group of assassins as he reined in his horse at a public house.

Cartwright had already received £3,000 by subscription from other merchants and manufacturers for the spirited defence of his mill. It has been estimated that 4,000 troops were now stationed in Yorkshire to put down this violence (for even after Horsfall's murder the arsenal of the Sheffield militia was attacked and shots were fired by workers in Leeds and Huddersfield). One of the workers involved at Rawfolds turned King's Evidence, and three men were hung drawn and quartered at York Castle for the murder of Horsfall. In the same period, sixty-three of the men who took part in the raid on Cartwright's Mill were tried. Seventeen were executed and six transported to Australia.

Actual violence gave way to intense political agitation. In this, Leeds gradually came to the fore as a centre of opinion. This was not so much because it was extreme but rather because in it there was a greater mix of opinion, more opportunity for compromise,

a more flexible response to issues. The employment of children
was a great scandal in Leeds, but it was not the only one. Workers
could be tried for conspiracy if they tried to combine or collabor-
ate for better wages. The workhouse system was a disgrace and
the houses known as Bastilles. From them there flowed unending
stories of beatings, cruelties, starvation. The critics who pooh-
poohed were silenced in 1846 when it was revealed that in the
Andover workhouse the inmates had been reduced by starvation
to eating the bones they were set to crush.

Short hours were an issue, the Poor Law an issue, Chartism an
issue. Unrepresented in Parliament, unrepresented locally, under
threat from the magistrates and in servitude to the millowners, the
population of Leeds in the first forty years of the nineteenth
century was in an impossible situation. It was an immigrant
population, pulled into new and strange surroundings by the
need to work and kept there by the necessity of the whole family
working. A healthy child was not so much an object of pride as
the actual salvation of his parents. A sick child was a curse on his
father. Religion was almost as confused in its relief as everything
else. The Hammonds quote a page of the *Leeds Independent* for
1819 in which side by side are two announcements, one for a
Reform meeting on Hunslet Moor, the other a Methodist
gathering at Skipton which was to assemble to pass the resolu-
tion: "That this meeting deeply deplores the religious and moral
state of the world, but especially of the Pagans, Mahommedans,
and Jews."

Methodism and the other dissenting religions took a great hold
in Yorkshire. In Leeds Nonconformism flourished and to it the
city owes its desire for independent action, its interest in education
and some at least of its bloody-mindedness. At the same time, the
religion that taught people to ignore their actual condition on
earth in expectation of a reward in Heaven was in contradiction
to the advice of Oastler, the Church of England Tory, who was
advising them to take their chance there and then. The rival claims
made Leeds a political centre of unusual complexity.

The factory system, as well as throwing simple people into
horrific situations in the way we have seen, also threatened the
livelihoods of the small middle men who had formed so much of
the wealth of the eighteenth-century town. The small craftsmen,

the highly skilled independent workers, the shopkeepers and the men with just a little property or investment, resented the great mills for the threat they offered them. These men were part of the great dream that Johnson had caught in his aphorism about the merchant. For them the manufacturer was no less a monster than for the hands. When the unrecorded, unsung hands vented their anger on the mills and the machinery it was in blind terror. The next stage of agitation involved men who could read a newspaper, write a letter, speak in public. Leeds had its full complement of them—indeed Leeds was only as rich as it was because of them.

What was happening to unfortunate Leeds was something quite foreign to the country as a whole, and without precedent in its history. You could not have a stouter champion of radical causes than Cobbett, and Cobbett said of manufacture, "I never like to see machines lest I should be tempted to endeavour to understand them." That was a good joke among Cobbett's darlings, the rural workers, but would have gone down badly on Hunslet Moor. The machines and the mills would not go away by wishing. All the legislation of the period is clearly bemused by the new conditions of the manufacturing towns.

Something alien to English ways was being forced into life in the industrial North. The irritation of the small tradesmen of Leeds must have been intense. They had helped raise Leeds to a position as honourable and secure as any market town in the nation, only to see it ruined in the space of forty years. It is as though in all the smoke and smother of the period 1800 to 1840 Leeds had to learn how to reassert its essential Englishness. Not until Victoria's visit in 1859 did it completely achieve that, just as it was not until the Great Exhibition that the Industrial Revolution was vindicated.

This dissociation from the traditional England, a feeling of foreignness, of alien character, certainly exists in the papers and speeches of the day. Has it also entered deep in the Leeds character and helped create that suspicion of the rest of the country that still exists? Certainly no other children in the world have been treated as Leeds children were treated in the worst times of the nineteenth century. Is that something that is easily forgotten?

There is one other thing. The old John Bull England was founded on lusty beef-eating strength, but shadowed by

indifference. This indifference expressed itself in complete un-
concern for the many. Men were hung for stealing a bunch of
radishes, or handkerchiefs from a washing line. Not only did their
fellows question nothing, they tolerated the public gibbet in the
market square, or at the crossroads, fought cocks in the shadow
of the corpse, killed and were killed with a strange kind of
equanimity. The poor, the blind and the mad were a backcloth
to town life that passed unremarked. Great wealth and great
poverty existed side by side and no one thought to find that
strange. Violence was epidemic and inexplicable when it did break
out. The English were an aggressive, pugnacious, tough set of
people, but conditioned to extremes of wealth and squalor a
foreigner found appalling.

That kind of England never returned. Leeds and the other
manufacturing towns were resented for their refusal to be counted
as traditional communities in the English pattern and doubly
resented for the ideas of progress they forced the rest of England to
accept. That progress was not just the material progress steam
ushered in, but also a sense of justice towards the many, a concern
for health and welfare, higher standards, new principles and ideals.
We can see the chagrin of conservative thinkers at the new, unwanted problems of industrialization. In time we can see also
emerging the recognition that what was happening in Leeds was
a lesson for the whole of England. The new English spirit was
born in the furnace heat of towns like Leeds.

V

VICTORIANS

WE MUST look now at some of the institutions that arose in the city in the last century. Their purposes were not always in perfect harmony. Some of them have died and are no more than paper, some of them are dying now. Some of them are stronger than they have ever been, great oaks from acorns planted with a proud flourish and a speech or two in great-grandfather's day.

There is a great deal which a book like this must leave out altogether, and absolutely no assurance that what is put on one side was not the most important thing in the world to someone then. Perhaps for many Victorians life revolved round the Assembly Rooms with their concerts of music by such as Jenny Lind, walks with father to the Archery Grounds, visits in high summer to the Bear Pits at Headingley, dances and concerts given by the gallant young sprigs of the Leeds Volunteers, or simply the dreary routine of church on Sundays, samplers, and drawing lessons in the long afternoons. The re-creation of that life needs a novelist to bring it to life, something the Victorians themselves took enormous pleasure in trying to do. It would need to be a pretty considerable novelist to avoid the clichés the period fashioned for itself. We must let those particular ghosts rest.

This is not the chapter either to review the political life of Leeds as it is told in the doings of its mayors and aldermen. Something between the two is called for, between the hard truths of the order book, the cash register and the chairman's gavel on the one hand and the teacups and gossip of long afternoons on the other. There are in fact a number of institutions which do fall into this middle ground. They are interesting today because of the aspirations they reveal. Almost without exception these were peculiarly Northern in character. The particular character of Northerners took a few remarkable twists in the new Leeds

driving forwards. In fact, a good deal of what is thought of as
time-honoured is hardly a hundred years old and was made in the
complicated, mazy history of middle-class Leeds.

There are some obvious household names to recall, men who
were known to the least as well to the greatest in the city. Who
had not heard in Leeds of Benjamin Gott, or John Marshall? It
was their mills which were such mighty employers of labour,
their machinery that was the wonder of all who saw it. Gott's
Bean Ing Mills in Wellington Street were fifty-four bays long and
the largest ever seen in the woollen trade. Gott had been apprenticed to the old merchant system; by the time he was thirty he
had the largest labour force ever assembled in the trade. Marshall
inherited from his father, looked around, saw the possibilities in
machine-spinning flax, created an industry where there was none.
Gott for wool and Marshall for flax: how often their names
cropped up on prospectuses, programmes, in company accounts
and in the columns of the newspapers. Sometimes the rest of the
city must have seemed to dance around these two men.

Sir George Head toured the North of England in the summer
of 1835. He seems to have visited the great millowners in their
place of work. In a significant passage of the book he later wrote,
he makes them out a respectful blank cheque:

> The public . . . have been slow to do justice to the character of the
> manufacturer, or appreciate the manifold difficulties of his position.
> Instead of regarding him as an individual on whom hundreds, nay,
> thousands of his fellow creatures depend for their daily bread, expres-
> sions of morbid sympathy have, on the contrary, never ceased to
> paint the situation of the operatives far darker than it is in reality;
> while there can be no doubt but that the well being of both parties
> has been preserved through the struggle, not alone by the industry of
> the servant, but by the benevolence of the master.

Head appears to have stayed in Leeds not much more than a
week. He never returned. Perhaps even Gott and Marshall had
more reservations than this about the society the machines and
the factories were creating. Their distinguished visitor was
especially scathing about interventionist philanthropy—the mis-
guided zeal of men and women who actually pointed out to
operatives their real plight. He believed instead in what he called
"the open channels" of sympathy and trust between master and

servant, taking it for granted that a servant wanted nothing more
than the chance to love his master as his father.

In Leeds, there was a certain amount of prudent insurance
against the possible breakdown of this genial arrangement. Head
had conveniently overlooked the scenes two years earlier when
1,000 ungrateful servants of the Leeds masters had picketed the
Scarborough Hotel, where the Factory Commissioners had hid-
den themselves away. Only two flags were carried by the pickets,
one of them an immense banner showing the scene at Water Lane
(where Marshall had his mill) at five o'clock in the morning—
clocking-on time for the children of six and upwards on whom
Marshall and all the rest depended. After torchlit speeches, half a
dozen miserable child labourers were carried into the Hotel to
meet the commissioners. It was to be another fifteen years before
the hours of such children were reduced to a mere ten a day. The
contemporary estimate of their life-span was put at twenty-four
years.

These matters were fiercely debated in the newspapers, and it is
there we must turn first. There was a long newspaper tradition in
Leeds, which had been a regional centre of printing since the days
of Queen Anne. The *Leeds Mercury* was started in 1718. It failed
for a while between 1755–67 but was operated again with moderate success. In 1801, a Preston printer named Edward Baines
acquired it from his previous employers, Binns and Brown.
Baines was twenty-seven. His family and the *Mercury* were to be
everywhere in Leeds for almost a century. Baines was a Member
for Leeds before Reform. His son, Edward junior, was Member
between 1859–74. Between them they made their paper one of
the most influential in the North of England for people of a
moderate cast of mind. Their editorship spanned the old and the
new, the father a conscientious man spelled by the princely
powers of the millowners, the son knighted for his services to
Gladstonian Liberalism.

They had their rivals. The *Leeds Intelligencer* was founded in
1754 and was destined to become in time the *Yorkshire Post*. Under
Kemplay it was the organ of the Tory-radicals, with this to say
about Baines senior in the eighteen-twenties: "The portly pro-
prietor of the Mercury—the sexagenarian dandy of Briggate—
the Solon of Leeds Workhouse . . . the Demosthenes of Hunslet

—is still the same poverty stricken adventurer that he was thirty years ago when he came into Leeds . . . his head as empty of ideas as his back was bare of clothes."

He is in fact a difficult man to place. The very name was enough to drive some men into rage, yet he considered himself a reformer, although a temperate one. It was the *Mercury* which campaigned for reform of the old parochial system of local government. He promoted the Leeds Savings Bank, founded the Public Baths, started the Temperance and Literary Societies, campaigned for the removal of civil disabilities, especially those directed against Dissenters. He was an absolute mine of information about Leeds business and trade and published a massive two-volume *History, Directory & Gazetteer of the County of York* in 1822 when he was in the thick of editing, politicking, and raising eleven children.

Baines wrote his *Directory* when the affairs of the town were conducted from the vestry of the church, as much as by the corporation. The lords of the manor still held a Court Leet, there was a daily egg and poultry market at the top of Briggate and the biggest building belonging to the public was the new court house and prison, at the botton of Park Row. In his introduction to the section of the *Directory* devoted to Leeds, he mentions only eight 'principal streets'. The Marshall family had not yet turned its attention to flax, but it was already clear enough that Leeds was going to have a giant's strength. It is not surprising that Baines the reformer was half-hypnotized by Baines the right man in the right place at the right time. He would have been a strange man not to fall under the spell of the great mercantile princes, who left to their own devices would have turned Leeds into one vast factory for which the few could feel pride and the many gratitude.

The *Intelligencer* rallied the opposition. It spoke for the men of more modest means, the thinking men who were not at the centre of power, but on its margins. To manage the great awakening giant a whole new social order was being forced into existence, men who took as their leaders Sadler and Oastler, and later on the indefagitable 'Owd Doctor', Walter Farquhar Hook, Vicar of Leeds; or James Hole, the social reformer. These men, the Tory reformers, were implacable in their opposition to the Whigs, had the sense to realize that the city would blow itself to pieces if the rich became richer and the poor any poorer. They met their enemies in committee, on the streets, and in some of the institutions we must look at now.

The Leeds Library was founded in 1768. The town was certainly in serious need of its service. The only public source of books and knowledge was the grammar school, where there was a collection that had been started with great vigour in 1692. The school library was not for the pupils but for any gentleman of the town who could make use of it. We can get some idea of how it had developed in the eighteenth century by the events of 1780, when accumulated funds set aside for the purchase of books were used by the master to build himself a new house.

There had, however, been an impressive private library in the town a generation earlier. Ralph Thoresby's *Ducatus Leodensis*, published in 1715, was the bringing together of this great man's scholarship. Thoresby was one of those unusual men who devotes his whole life and all his intelligence to a history of the place in which he was born. He was an incurable, chronic amateur of knowledge. His style is a mixture of invaluable fact and high-table elegance, rather like dining with an absent-minded don. Speaking of the building of St. John's, consecrated in 1634, Thoresby says, with characteristic elegance: "It then pleased God to move the heart of this great and good magistrate (John Harrison 1579–1658) to build this noble and stately church so that the inhabitants, who before complained with the children of the Prophets 'the place where we dwell is too strait for us' may now say 'Rehoboth, God has made room for us'."

John Harrison built and endowed the church entirely from his own pocket. He was the son of a rich cloth merchant from Pawdmyre, in Leeds. It is entirely in keeping with Thoresby's attractive personality that he knew of the existence of a memorial tablet at Harrison's birthplace and was a curious bystander when "it was sunk below the pavement as a supposed nuisance" but forgets to mention exactly where this took place. It was possibly in Lower Briggate.

Harrison had built the grammar school a permanent home in a field he owned between Briggate and Vicar Lane, opposite St. John's. Until that benefaction, the school had shifted about, blown this way and that by the wills and bequests of earlier benefactors. It stayed in the field Harrison found for it until 1859, when it moved to its present position at the bottom of Woodhouse Moor. The school was walled around and appears to have had only slightly more dignity than a barn. Until Lawson enlarged it at the time of the library mentioned earlier, there was no form of flooring and no hearth. Lawson thoughtfully added that. The school remained extremely cold, had as many mice in it as pupils, and was, until the commencement of the Leeds Library, the only public supply of knowledge in the town. You have to imagine tetchy old men climbing to the upper room, where the library was housed, and rooting round in the shelves in a filthy temper, while children screamed and cheered underneath.

The Leeds Library came into being on a new wave of enthusiasm for learning. The town's booksellers were prominent in its establishment. One of them, Binns, was the founder of the printers who later on bought the *Mercury*. His shop has been described as "probably the nearest approximation in Leeds at that time to a university". A colleague, one Ogle, gave part of his premises to the new library, and became the first librarian. The scheme of the library was simple. It was a subscription library on the lines of those being set up in other large towns. Membership was at that time unlimited at one guinea. The annual subscription was 5s. The library was to be open from ten a.m. until four p.m. Books purchased for the patrons were never to be sold.

The early business meetings of the new library were attended by the new minister of Mill Hill Chapel, the dynamic young Joseph Priestley. Mill Hill had been one of the first Dissenting meeting houses erected in the North after the General Indulgence and was built in 1673. Even after its opening persecution of Dissenters was sufficiently commonplace to send any man to jail who refused to give the 'Oxford Oath', and the 'schismaticks', as they were called, were not complety safe until the Toleration Act of 1689. The ubiquitous Thoresby was a subscriber at Mill Hill (as well as worshipping in the Anglican communion at St. Michael's and St. Peter's) only ten years after the former minister had been tossed into Newgate for his opinions. Thoresby himself had married the granddaughter of one of the leading Quakers, an old lady called Grace Sykes, while Grace herself was locked up in York Castle.

This was old history when Priestley arrived in Leeds. He was

Back-to-backs scheduled for demolition

the product of the Dissenting Academies, a Fellow of the Royal Society for his work on electricity, a Doctor of Letters of the University of Edinburgh, a theologian and a scientist. His dynamism and scholarship endeared him to the library. He became their first secretary and their second president. By 1781, the book stock over Ogle's shop had grown to the extent that it was forcing the poor man out of house and home. The library took itself off to Ibbetson's house, in Kirkgate. When that was unsatisfactory, the proprietors were forced to issue shares and raise by subscription sufficient funds to buy their own premises. This they did in 1807 on a site "in the new road about to be constructed from Briggate to Albion St."; and there the library remains to this day. In 1813 the membership was limited to 500 shares. These and many other regulations have remained unchanged. To its fortunate subscribers, the Leeds Library is an enviable oasis of Regency calm over a shoe shop in Commercial Street. Some of the present book has been written there.

In recent times no library in Yorkshire has had a more scholarly servant than Frank Beckwith, M.A., the late librarian. His knowledge of nineteenth century Leeds was a vast and compendious one and it is in tribute to his scholarship the following anecdote, which he first published from the records of the library, is included. In 1829 the *Leeds Monthly Magazine* came alongside the library and delivered this thunderous cannonade: "It is generally supposed that there are only two infallible personages alive, viz. The Pope of Rome and the Duke of Wellington; but this must be a mistake. If we may be allowed to judge from circumstances, we are certainly of the opinion that the gentlemen who form the Committee of the Leeds Library have also a very fair claim to this distinction."

The article goes on to outline recent purchases by the committee, which include "A life of Lady Maxwell, by the Revd. John Lancaster (a piece of dull evangelical biography, of which article there is surely too much already) ... and ... The Journals of the House of Commons (in eighty immense volumes, ordered merely to fill up some bottom shelves)." The piece concludes with a list of those things the committee decided against stocking, ending with the *Leeds Monthly Magazine*.

The Leeds Philosophical and Literary Society was founded in

5

The crest of Briggate looking towards the river

1819, the foundation stone being laid by Benjamin Gott. Baines was its begetter. The Philosophical Hall built by Chantrell was not pulled down until 1965, when it made way for the new Midland Bank in Park Row. It had a similar effect to the library, magnetizing the intelligentsia of the city to it, mixing learning and a simple appetite for the curious that made its public museum a place of wonder. In time, prehistoric skeletons from the coal measures mingled with Egyptian mummies and a stuffed Bengali tiger. (The tiger was blown to pieces with many other exhibits by a stray German bomb in March 1941.) The society bequeathed its museum to the city in 1921, but much more important perhaps than the content of the Philosophical Hall was its remarkable acoustics. It was reputed to be the best place for music in Leeds. Elgar, Holst, Vaughan Williams and Beecham conducted there. The Leeds Philharmonic met there regularly from 1880 until the building was demolished.

White lists the principal cultural facilities of the city at 1853. As well as the Philosophical and Literary Society, he mentions the Music Union and Choral Society and the Leeds Academy of Art. As well as the Leeds Library, he lists no fewer than twenty-two subscription or circulating libraries. There were three theatres —the Royal, Princess's, and Royal Casino, as well as the music-hall. As well as the Philosophical Society's museum, there was a private one opened by Mr. Calvert, of Commercial Street. White put the number of week-day schoolchildren at 8,000, "and a much larger number on Sundays". The School of Design had been opened by the Government seven years earlier.

We have seen how the development of an eighteenth-century town of quality was arrested and then destroyed by the rise of the manufacturing industries. It was customary in the early years of the century to speak with admiration of the busy streets and curious machinery and then leave by the first available train, as Sir George Head had done. The people who were left behind were forced by circumstances to consider schemes of improvement, some of them intended merely to make the place bigger or faster, some of them of a genuine reforming character. The library and the Philosophical Hall were the meeting ground for the men who had either of these in mind. They are a reflection of an independent spirited people left to their own devices in a revolutionary situation, without the patronage of the great aristocratic families, or its alternative, powerful central government. You made your way to the places we have mentioned through a year-round industrial haze, past workshops which blazed light and heat, or by mills which gave an uncomfortable idea of barracks or prisons. You might carry in your hat some improving notions to be read aloud to an audience of men like yourself, but you would be conscious all the time of your work, the pull of your trade upon your life. It would be wrong to see the things we have mentioned merely as the occupations of leisure. They were not.

In fact, Leeds had coined a word for the sort of 'improvements' it spoke of so frequently and so earnestly. The phrase 'self-help' was first used in Leeds by Samuel Smiles when he was editing the *Leeds Times*. "By far the best part of what is doing for the people of Leeds is being done *by themselves*. The help of patronage is good, but self-help is infinitely better. . . ." Smiles meant by this the sort of help working men could get by co-operation between themselves, but his words applied equally to the members of his own class. Self-help was an ideal which was founded on a practical reality. Unless Leeds helped itself, it was unlikely to get help another way. The key to the whole complex social inbalance was education. Since the Victorians did not understand the significance of children, when they spoke of education they very often meant their own.

The first paper ever presented to the Literary Institute was "On the diffusion of knowledge among the middle classes". In 1842 the institute merged with the Mechanics' Institute, which was then already twenty years old. The Mechanics' Institute perfectly sums up the spirit of the age. Founded to teach working men the new science and technology it had rapidly become dominated in Leeds by the more radical of the middle classes. It was exceptionally lucky to attract the services of James Hole.

The general aims of the institutes were "to make the man a better mechanic and the mechanic a better man". West Riding Institutes federated in 1837. Hole gave his time to both the Leeds Institute and what became the Yorkshire Union. He held office in both. He was a Londoner who came to Leeds when he was in his twenties. He worked as a confidential clerk for a worsted merchant and lived in the city for twenty-five years. When he

left in 1867 he found that forever after he would be known as
'Mr. Hole of Leeds' in tribute to years he had spent in caring for
practically ever aspect of the working man's education and
welfare. He was gifted with what his age called 'practical philan-
throphy', that was, in his case, a sort of coats-off democratic
socialism. Hole gave his unstinted support to every sensible
measure then being canvassed for a better society and became in
his later years, on the basis of his work in Leeds, a sort of father
figure to nationally canvassed social welfare programmes.

He found Leeds a fairly radical centre of opinion on his arrival.
There were in the city many dozens of men of middle means who
had largely taught themselves. One of the first places Hole turned
to after his introduction to these men at the Mechanics' Institute
was the Leeds Redemption Society. The society was founded in
1845 and took as its starting point pretty well wholesale rejection
of the industrial society that had developed since the century
began. If this sounds like early communism, it was partway the
case. The men who gathered at Mill Hill on Sunday afternoons
had before them the glowing example of Robert Owen.

The life of Owen was a classic of the new industrial wealth and
power. The son of a saddler from Newtown, in Montgomery-
shire, he was apprenticed at ten to a Stamford draper. When he
was fourteen, Owen moved to Manchester to complete his
apprenticeship. The town was in a boom. Owen borrowed £100
and forced his way into machine-manufacture. Before he was
twenty he was managing a cotton mill which employed 500 hands.
By the time he was twenty-eight, he had moved to the New
Lanark Mills, the biggest in Scotland, negotiated its takeover,
married the outgoing boss's daughter and was the best-known
factory manager in the nation. The story had just about every
virtue in it that counted—luck, drive, thrift, commercial genius,
a touch of ruthlessness, the pleasing sentiments of a good marriage.
There was more to come.

If Owen had settled for the respect of his own class at New
Lanark, the world would have heard no more of him. But he was
an unusual man in more than one particular. Owen was a thinking
man whose thought was at root religious. There was nothing
wrong with that either, if he had confined his religion to Sundays.
Owen did not. For twenty-five years he harped on one theme at

New Lanark, that of an entirely new industrial order, based on full participation of everyone in the plant. He fathered co-operation as a principle, going much further than consumer co-operation (although the Rochdale Pioneers were undoubtedly inspired by his ideas). He did his practical best to make a fully co-operative industrial society, at any rate inside the gates of his own mill. The wrath and contempt of other owners poured down on his head.

The Leeds Redemption Society took Owenism even further: "We intend to unite the labour of all for the benefit of all. In our operations we shall recognize no landlord, no capitalist, no labourer, as separate individuals having separate interests; but all will be landlords, all capitalists, all labourers." The men who put this point of view were not revolutionary students but clerks, small shopkeepers, printers, tradesmen, teachers. They were the product of the system, not its open enemy. They dressed like everyone else in Leeds, they went to the same churches and chapels, they walked their children over the same moor as everyone else.

What is more, they had the grit to make it work. Having issued the prospectus (always the most popular moment of revolution) they took off their coats and set about doing what they preached. They asked for weekly subscriptions of not less than a penny to buy land for a new experimental community where their ideas could bear fruit. Like Hole, they were men who really worked for change, nor only as Redemptionists, but in organizing the co-operative flour mill they set up in competition with a mono-poly, in designing improved housing for workers, in lecturing at the Mechanics' Institute.

In his brilliant monograph on Hole, J. F. C. Harrison follows the fortunes of the Redemptionists. By 1847 the society had enough money to acquire a poor farm in Carmarthen, at a place called Garnlwyd. Fourteen men and their families actually went from the back streets of Leeds and set up a commune in remote Wales. Local children collected wild blackberries and sold them for a shilling a basket to the commune, who turned them into jam and sent the jars off back to Leeds. The Redemptionists had set up a co-operative in Trinity Street to retail the produce of the Garnlwyd farm.

There is something extremely moving about this story of the blackberry jam from Wales. The co-operative store in Trinity Street which sounded so grand in reports and minutes was actually a tiny room over a stables, organized and worried over by men who were not themselves working class. In Wales, the commune was struggling along with land that had deterred other farmers from bothering with that particular bit of marshy, infertile country. By 1855 the Redemption Society was dead. The shop closed. The farmers stayed just where they were. There was so much else to be done in Leeds. Perhaps for years the middle-class larders of Hole and his friends would contain a jar or two of jam as souvenir of the men and women from Leeds who went to found a perfect society eight miles from Swansea.

Men like Hole and his friend Egglestone, joining hands with the orthodox Tories like Dr. Hook, slowly filled in the great gaps which had yawned between master and hand. Hole was an incredible man whose 'practical philanthropy' covered the fields of adult education, consumer co-operation, community development, social welfare, housing, even industrial arbitration. He opposed the old pattern of *laissez faire* liberalism of men like Baines, Gott, and Marshall with a dozen different schemes of practical socialism. It is one of the curiosities of Leeds intellectual life that he was able to do all this sitting in committee alongside Anglicans, like Dr. Hook, or establishment figures like the younger Baines.

Just as the century had started with the cry of work, work, yet again work, in its middle years it was moved most by the word education. The education of the new middle class in Leeds was for Hole and those lucky enough to know him a radical, questioning one. He himself was only unique for the number of interests he had. He could count on many more who shared the same general sympathy. Smiles was right about self-help. It was much more than a cynical invitation to those who had nothing to climb a greasy pole. It was something very deep in the experience of his own class.

Perhaps the opening of the town hall by the Queen was a kind of watershed for such men. Quite apart from the fact that the mills had all closed for the day for almost the first time in nearly sixty years, this was the first visit to the city of a reigning monarch.

It seemed that the visit marked more than one first. It was the first time Leeds had lifted its eyes from the loom and the bench and looked around. It had felt pain, and now it learned how to feel pride.

After the ecstasies of the Queen's visit, Leeds broadens and thickens. Its prosperity depended on more extensive and subtle forms of industry and commerce and the river broadened, so to speak. The old institutions changed their character and new ones came into crowd the scene. Some of the old rivalries and factions lost their urgency. Hole went to London to become the organizing secretary of the Associated Chambers of Commerce. Hook was never offered a bishopric, as he might have expected, but left Leeds to become Dean of Chichester the year following the great events of the Queen's visit. Baines senior had died in 1848. His son was returned as M.P. the year Dr. Hook took his farewell of the parish, and represented the city until 1874. He was knighted in 1880. Priestley's Mill Hill was demolished in 1847. Harrison's original grammar school became a foundry in 1859.

Perhaps the Forster Act of 1870 changed Leeds more than anything self-help could have accomplished. Universal education was the one reform which could quicken the broad, sluggish stream of Leeds life and drive it once again into a millrace. The 1870 Act provided it. The only improvement a great industrial city needs ultimately is education, as Leeds had known all along. Thirty-two thousand children had assembled from all the Sunday schools in Leeds to cheer Victoria as she passed to the town hall in her carriage. Their children, and their children's children, inherited what was denied to them.

In 1877 the ramshackle Yorkshire College moved from its ludicrously inadequate premises in Cookridge Street to a new site in Woodhouse Lane. On the left-hand side of the road there was a pleasant estate of modest villas known as Beech Grove. The Yorkshire College bought a plot for £13,000. As J. S. Fletcher put it with a sort of broadbottomed complacency in 1900 "the charm of the surroundings gives it something of the air of quiet ease and antiquity observable about the Colleges of the old University towns . . .". Poor Beech Grove, to have harboured such a monster. Hardly one stone stands on another of what was a quiet, pleasant, residential neighbourhood. The cuckoo conquered. Beech Grove had let into its streets the buzzing little chick of what was swiftly to become the University of Leeds.

The railways had done as much as anything to settle prosperity on Leeds. Henry Clarkson of Wakefield, whom we have already met, was employed by Stephenson to survey part of the Leeds–Derby line in 1835. Before a service could be opened a Bill had to pass through Parliament. In the committee stages of these bills all the owners, lessees and occupiers of land along the proposed route had to give their assent. The canvassing of these interested parties was conducted face to face, and not by post. Clarkson was once sent by road to Birmingham to get the agreement of a man who owned a pigsty in Hunslet. To make a good story better, the owner of the pigsty was a commercial traveller. When Clarkson at last tracked down his lodgings in Birmingham the man had gone to Warwick. The frantic round trip took Clarkson four days.

The 'railway mania' that had seized England was incredible. The first steam locomotive tests took place at Rainhill, on a completed section of the Manchester and Liverpool Railway. The Company had offered a £500 prize for the successful steam loco and there were finally three competitors: Braithwaite's *Novelty*, Hackworth's *Sans Pareil*, and Stephenson's *Rocket*. We know the result, of course. In the next year Stephenson built a further eight engines of the same pattern. In the next ten years Parliament sanctioned the building of over 2,000 miles of railway. The boom was fast and furious. In 1846 alone Parliament approved proposals worth £132 millions. This represented only a quarter of all the schemes submitted in a helter-skelter of speculation. Six hundred thousand men were employed on building railways as fast as investors could get their prospectuses together.

The first railway into Leeds was the Leeds and Selby, floated in 1829, immediately after the *Rocket* trials, given the Royal Assent in June 1830. Gott, Marshall and Baines were among the original subscribers who bought shares at £100 each. Irish labour poured into Leeds to commence the work—men already noted for their terrifying violence as much as their great strength and skill in navigation. The navvies came to town with a vengeance. At one

Victorian well-to-do housing, Headingley
Overleaf: The Meanwood Valley, looking south

period, one man in every twenty was Irish—the first real immigration in Leeds.

The company had before it the passionate advocacy of railways from a source near at home. Young George Hudson of York was already a byword for railway mania of a kind that thrilled and later on ruined many a man with a bit of capital to invest. When he was twenty-seven, Hudson, the humble linen-draper, inherited £30,000. He put the lot into the North Midland and started to make a fortune. After his first five years, he opened his own bank. He became a director of the company and its presiding genius. He was notorious for his determination to force the railway through York, at any cost.

Unlike York, Leeds was a terminus. The Leeds and Selby began at Marsh Lane, which was described in 1835 as "one of the most unpleasant and dirty, but likely soon to become one of the most improving parts of the town of Leeds. The prodigious embankments upon which the Rail-Road is conducted from the Tunnel will excite the admiration of the visitor."

This tunnel was the product of the imported labour. Certainly it competed with Marshall's Mill for the admiration of all who saw it. The new technology was nothing if not large in scale. The tunnel was 700 yards long and bricklined throughout. That impressed. A hole in the hill treated with as much finish as went into a workman's house. Greater finish, taking into account the arch-work and specialist brickwork. The tunnel had the pleasing effect of taking passengers from Marsh Lane and its miseries and bringing them in astonishment to the agricultural beauties of Halton, "the waving woods of Temple Newsam and the pleasing plantations of Killingbeck". At Surton and Garforth the line passed the first coalpits. Their owners were of course proprietors of the new line. At Aberford the railway came in sight of its destination, across a valley which Fuller describes the Bishop of Durham explaining to Henry VIII as "the richest that he ever found in all his travails through Europe. For within ten miles of Hesselwood, the seat of Vavasors, there were 165 manor houses of Lords, Knights and Gentlemen of the best quality."

So it had been in 1548 when the bishop advised his king from the back of a horse, reined in under a tree. Now, thanks to a colossal tunnel which represented a piece of civil engineering the

Victorian pieties

like of which had never before been seen, the new industrial power spilled out over this ancient source of landed wealth.

The railway was partially opened to the public on Monday, 22nd September 1834. One hundred and sixty passengers were pulled along by *Nelson*, watched by over twenty thousand amazed citizens. The whole length of the line was attended by the curious and the apprehensive. In what had been distant Temple Newsam, there was particular amazement, as Leeds came bursting out of its valley. The journey out was delayed, to add to the drama, "in consequence of the axles of the engine being too large"; but on the triumphant return journey *Nelson* did the distance in an unbelievable hour and four minutes.

In the first four days of novelty, the Leeds and Selby carried 779 passengers at a cost of 3s. a first-class seat, 2s. for an open carriage. The through fare to Hull, by steamer connection, cost only another 2s., an indication of the intentions of the proprietors to recoup their outlay. Even a dog was charged a shilling—but what excitement for a dog! What excitement for everybody as the most sudden 'improvement' Leeds had seen came bursting and rumbling, clattering and puffing to a world far from Briggate, but now a part of it.

Commercial traffic on the railway had yet to commence. The real pay-off had yet to begin. After all, the track still had a tarmacadam bed for horse to pull the goods freights, and had not the *Encyclopaedia Britannica* warned in 1824: "It will appear that this species of inland carriage is principally applicable where trade is considerable and the length of conveyance short. . . . It is only in particular circumstances that navigation with the aid either of locks or inclined planes to surmount the elevations will not present a more convenient medium for extended trade."

That was a point of view likely to be quoted often by the canal companies. The railways were a speculation, but of a kind that taught men who knew nothing of it an entirely new range of skills and principles. Anyone with common sense could run a canal. A railway posed new problems, not only while it was being built, but in its management and particularly in its engineering development. For Leeds, the widening of these skills turned out to be crucial.

The early days of railway found a tremendous shortage of

engineers to build the locomotives. Each engine was in fact custom-made. Each engine had bolts and parts specially made for it by the engineer and his mechanics. There were no standardized fixings and no particular measurements made of any fine workings. Stephenson was king because he was out on his own: the future of the railway was in his head as much as on any drawing board. Engineering tolerances were a matter of sticking with the brute once it had been constructed, and if it would not go as designed, patiently fiddling it into life. If a bolt sheared, there was no stock item to replace it. The mechanic made another one like the first, and made it fit by trial and error.

The country had in fact to make a machine-tool industry for the age of steel. The planing machine and the lathe came in the eighteen-twenties, the steam hammer in the 'thirties, the punch drill in the 'forties. Whitworth's of Manchester, Fox of Derby and Matthew Murray of Leeds became front-running firms not just because they were founded by engineers but because round them was growing the tool and machine-tool industry on which engineering development depended. It is James Watt's statue in City Square, but his rival Murray made Leeds famous for engineering. This fame was international. In 1841 the French built a flax factory entirely from Leeds machines and serviced exclusively by Leeds mechanics.

The crash that had to come in railway shares did not hurt Leeds as much as it might have done. Its capital was more widely invested. The statue of James Watt in City Square should be a source of profound indignation to any true son of Leeds. Watt, to any friend of Leeds, was nothing less than an industrial spy and plagiarist, genius though he may be to the rest of England. The man whose ideas he stole was Matthew Murray. Without Murray Leeds might have faltered. It is still the only city in the country where a man will say in a pub, in all seriousness, that he was cheated by Watt, a controversy all of 120 years old.

Murray was the only voter on the 1807 electoral roll described as 'engineer'. He was, in complete accuracy, the father of Leeds engineering. Born at Stockton in 1765, he came searching for work in Leeds when he was twenty-three. Because of his skill as an engine fitter, he was taken on by Marshall. The 'Round Foundry' in Holbeck which he set up next to the Marshall Mill was a source of great interest, for it was grasped by all his competitors that Murray was very much more than an engine-wright. Before his death in 1826, he had developed or taken out original patents for machines to do with flax-spinning, carding, pumping and air-pumping, locomotive engineering, cylinder boring and pressure gauges. He lit the Round Foundry and some streets round about with his own gasworks. All this was the source of the greatest interest—and jealousy.

The Grand Prince of all the Russias visited Murray at his works and gave the engineer a diamond ring in recognition of his skill. Like Stephenson, Murray was a self-taught man, without formal education of any kind. He was the precursor of a breed of English engineers later on to become a byword on the continent. Among his many visitors to the works was Watt. Murray freely showed him his plant and technical drawings. But when Murray and his wife repaid the visit to Watt, the perfidious man refused to let them into the works at all, and turned them away with the barest civility. Even worse, Robert Watt secretly negotiated the purchase of Camp Field next to the Roundy Foundry, in order to prevent Murray from expanding. It was empty and undeveloped for years.

Fenton, Murray and Jackson, Todd, Kitson and Laird. From these original engineering works there proliferated the extensive complex of machine-tool manufacture that Leeds enjoyed in the great expansionist days after 1850. In 1862 the old Murray foundry was retitled the Victoria. Under the direction of the engineers Smith, Beacock and Tannent, it became a magnet to anyone interested in learning engineering. Krupps sent his sons there. The best of the foremen, men like Cryer, the Heaton brothers and Thomas Jackson started teaching mechanical drawing and engineering principles at the Mechanics' Institute and moved on to become distinguished engineers in their own right.

Kitson himself was pupil of the Mechanics' Institute and the Literary Institute which later merged with it. The Airedale Foundry was set up by him in 1836. A hundred years later the Kitson family could claim one member of the House of Lords and another in the Commons. It had produced two Lord Mayors of Leeds and a Deputy-Lieutenant of the West Riding. Two of its womenfolk became J.P.s There was a President of the Institute

of Mechanical Engineers and a President of the Institute of Locomotive Engineers. Cambridge was the Kitson's University. Six
of the family took first-class honours there. The founder of this
dynasty had been a publican's son who was interested in anything
mechanical.

It is in this context that the Yorkshire College must be seen.
The idea for a college was originally mooted in 1868, when the
sum of £60,000 was canvassed for its commencement. It is not
really surprising in light of the education that men were getting
at the lathe and the bench that the idea languished for a few years
as a paper dream. In time the Clothmaker's Company helped out
and, with only £17,000 at its disposal, the College of Science
opened in 1874. It was hardly a mighty push forward. The college
was housed in an old bankruptcy court in Cookridge Street and
boasted four classrooms and a laboratory. There was also a shed
in the garden for 'noxious experiments'. One student turned up
on the first day and had to wait two days before he was joined
by a colleague. At the end of the first year the total strength of
the college was nineteen students, which was reckoned to be
'satisfactory'. In 1877, an arts professor was appointed, and the
college assumed its full title the following year.

James Kitson had been instrumental in setting the college in
motion. Baines junior had encouraged its progress. But before
we can follow it in its triumphant removal to the quiet haven of
Beech Grove, where we last left it, we must see how it had been
helped towards university status by the joining of forces with
another proud Leeds institution.

The teaching of medicine had been particularly advanced in
Leeds since 1831. In that year the local doctors banded together
to form a medical school which as it went along became nationally
famous, especially for its teaching of surgery. The school started
as a series of early morning lectures given in the dispensary before
the start of morning surgery. In 1833 it moved to East Parade
where the Yorkshire Bank stands now. Although the men who
organized the school were only ordinary doctors themselves, they
were in fact teaching medicine and training their successors. Until
the University of London admitted external candidates to its
degrees, in 1858, the Leeds doctors could confer no qualification
on their pupils. But when the infirmary was being built the

school moved to nearby Park Street and became the first purpose-built medical school in the country. In 1884 this honoured and famous institution amalgamated its teaching with that of the Yorkshire College.

We can now see the embryo of a university, with faculties of medicine, science, technology and arts. Arts fall last in the list because that was the importance placed on them then. It was true that the first principal of the college (and first Vice-Chancellor of the university) was an Oxford classics man, Nathan Bodington. But if he was especially sympathetic to the arts provision within his college, he had to grapple with a weird collection of interests, including the incorporated Leeds Ladies Educational Association of 1867. Nobody—not even an Oxford classicist—could live long in Leeds and not see what the purpose of a college was. It was to make progress, and to do that one made science.

Once snug behind its elms at Beech Grove, the college was admitted—with some pains—to the federal Victoria University in 1887. Victoria University was a deedy, wordy, unworkable answer to the problems of three colleges in Leeds, Manchester and Liverpool. The college had been opened on its new site by the Prince and Princess of Wales in 1885, when the Baines Memorial Wing and the central buildings were displayed for the first time. Baines had given £25,000 to his memorial wing, an act of considerable generosity as well as fervid patriotism. In 1894 Great Hall was opened by the Duke and Duchess of Kent. The speeches and the toasting were splendid occasions; it is difficult to remember that the whole place was not much larger in scope than a college of education today. The academic standards were various, to put it politely. Part-time students were desk by desk with the honours candidates. The town of Leeds was not unsuspicious of the intrusion of some high-minded staff who were 'not local', in the damning phrase. The Federal University was doomed from the start by the dramatic power and authority of its strongest member, Owens College, Manchester. Times were hard.

In 1903–4 the Victoria University broke down and Leeds sued the Privy Council for its own charter, which was granted, not without a spirited challenge from Sheffield for a Yorkshire Federal University which if it had succeeded would have ended the careers of Hull, York and Bradford before they began. At the inaugural congregation in 1904, honorary degrees were conferred on those who had given Leeds such dogged loyalty, including Sir James Kitson and Sir John Barran. Barran had been knighted for his services to the ready-made clothing industry, which he practically invented. Despite an appalling poem by the Poet Laureate, calling on the university to turn its attention to the arts, it was a good local occasion. It struck the same note as had been heard in 1858, when the Queen had visited the town.

The relationship between the university and the city was a difficult one, however. Life was by no means fulfilled at the inauguration ceremonies. Leeds had achieved university status long before it was ready for it in financial terms. There simply was not enough money about for the staff to do their job with any assurance. Experiments were conducted in chemistry and physics "as if the necessary equipment were available". More importantly, the Senate struggled for an idea of a university in the face of appalling problems of fund-raising. Not everyone was as generous as Baines and Kitson had been. Chasing money was the sole preoccupation of Bodington and his successor Sadler.

Sadler was a brilliant Oxford graduate, a gilded youth. For ten years he worked for the Board of Education and for another eight as professor of education in Manchester. He was full of charm, urbane, cultivated, heterodox in opinion. In other words he was something new in Leeds. He had hardly arrived when he was involved in a first-class row.

In 1913 there was a municipal strike in the city. It was December and the men wanted 2s. a week more. Left to itself and in ordinary circumstances, the strike might have been resolved quickly. Sadler, the new Vice-Chancellor of a still-new university took it on himself to encourage his students to break the strike by doing the necessary work, without pay, 'as a public duty'. His motive was simple and honourable, but for the time and place incredible. Sadler felt that where a public service was threatened, he was acting in the interests of the community as a whole by strike-breaking. He even emphasized that he did what he did without the slightest class antagonism. This curious incident was a long time remembered. In 1926 when Sadler's successor went to a trade union meeting in Leeds to ask for funds, he was asked directly and without hesitation how he had the cheek to ask for money for an institution which had broken the 1913 strike.

Before he left office, the unlucky Sadler was involved in another rift with the city. A friend persuaded him to commission the artist Eric Gill to carve a war memorial for those who had fallen in the Great War. Gill, who was an extraordinary man even for an Oxford man to deal with, seems to have had little trouble in completely dominating Sadler. When the sculptural panel was unveiled by the Bishop of Ripon in 1923, it showed Christ driving the moneylenders from the temple. The moneylenders wear contemporary clothes such as Leeds was famous for and they bore an unhappy resemblance to the average sort of citizen found on city councils. Few people shared Gill's sense of humour and most blamed Sadler. It is entirely to Sadler's credit that he waited until Gill was dead before revealing that the artist had changed the design during the commission and left the panel until it was too late for the university to alter it. His successor was very keen on growing ivy over this embarrassment. Students kept it well trimmed back. The whole sculpture can be seen today in the foyer to the Rupert Beckett Building, after its dignified removal from great hall.

Sadler was a brilliant and gifted Vice-Chancellor nevertheless. He filled the office at a time of great trouble for the university. In 1913–14, the total number of students was still under 700. When a boom in student numbers did occur, after the war, there was no capital to meet it. It is interesting that even in the early 'twenties, it was by no means certain that the university could continue. But in 1925 the jubilee of the old Yorkshire College coincided with the coming of age of the university. The time and the opportunity was as good as anything the Senate would ever get to pull itself into a secure harbour.

The new Vice-Chancellor, James Black Baillie, was an administrator with as much genius for what he himself called 'stones and lime' as Sadler had possessed spirit. A university appeal was launched in October 1935. Whatever else he was, Baillie proved to be a wizard at releasing money from the purses of rich men. When the Duke of York formally opened the appeal, there was already £175,000 in the bank, new capital worth a quarter of all

The Inner Ring Road as it plunges to the York Road

the assets the university had acquired in twenty-one years of troubled life.

From this period the familiar parts of the present university fall into place. Sir Edward Brotherton gave £100,000 towards the endowment of a library. Mr. W. Riley-Smith gave £25,000 to plans for a Union building. Finally, triumphantly, Frank Parkinson gave £200,000 for a building to house Brotherton's library and provide Senate and council with their true elegance of surroundings. The Brotherton was opened in 1936 by the Archbishop of Canterbury, in the presence of the Princess Royal and the Duchess of Devonshire. Lord Brotherton had seen the laying of the foundation stone but had died shortly after. It was then revealed that he had bequeathed a further £100,000 "for the general benefit of the University". He also bequeathed his own collection of books. It is housed in a special suite of rooms within the library he endowed.

The opening of the Brotherton was in March. In November of the same year Frank Parkinson wrote to Baillie to offer his gift of £200,000. The construction of 'The Parkinson' was delayed by the war and it was not formally opened until 1951. Parkinson had been a poor student in Leeds in the days of the college and had received a small Baines scholarship to help him through. His vast electrical business gave him in time the opportunity to repay in really princely terms the original opportunity he had gained at Leeds.

The names of the university's buildings are a roll-call of public endowment on a grand scale. Colonel Tetley's contributions exceeded £100,000. Brotherton's heir gave £50,000 in 1945 to endow a department of chemical engineering. Riley Smith the brewer, Montague Burton the clothing manufacturer, Beckett the banker—these are all local names. By the time the first fifty years had passed, the university's assets had risen from £11,400 to over £4 million.

Beech Grove had taken some severe knocks and a good deal of Portland Stone (a Leeds invention) was now present where red brick had been before. The end of a journey appeared to be in sight. In fact the journey was only just beginning. So much has happened in the last quarter-century that will change Leeds, so much that is epitomized by the almost completed development

6

Thornton's Arcade, Briggate

plans, we must take its story along with the rest of the city's future. We need to go back first to the city itself. We must look at the development of two particular districts of Leeds which show a contrast in their history, for in that contrast we can find new aspects of our portrait.

VI

HEADINGLEY

MOST of the manufacturing side of Leeds outlived the people who were involved in it. The lives of the factory hands were short and bitter. The machines they built and the mills that housed them easily outlived the human contact. It was the reverse of the situation today, when a man will quickly outlive the ideas current when he was born and new conditions, new organization, a whole new environment will engulf him. In the great expansionist days of Leeds, a beam engine might be serviced by two or three generations of mechanics. A son would follow his father at the same bench, or dragging the same load.

The old-town quality of Briggate clung until the last. It is in the nature of people to seek continuity with the past. Although 'new' was one of the most exciting words in the mouth in Leeds for a hundred years, 'ancient' was its most powerful antonym. The architecture of the new mills was often a copy of more 'ancient' styles. Marshall excelled himself in this. His mill was built 'in the Egyptian style', which would have been mystifying to dynastic Egypt but was sufficiently like to impress the whole of England when it was built. A novel touch was that provision was made for sheep to graze on the flat roof. Folk myth has it that this ingenious arrangement worked well until some of the flock fell through a fanlight into the machinery.

It was in the nature of the factory environment to destroy the natural order and keep sheep on the roof, just as it is the compensating nature of sheep to fall through the ceiling. However, the harsh truth was that anyone who saw that incident (if it ever happened) was dead within the running-in period of the machine he tended. Although so much happened that was progress, the style of it was not particularly elevating nor were the memorials of nineteenth-century progress anything to compare with the calm of Dales villages forsaken for the wealth of the town. The great merchants tried to establish squares and terraces on the London pattern—and we know by looking at Newcastle that it could be done. In Leeds it never really happened. The continuity that was needed to develop Leeds in the crucial period up until the completion of the town hall was never created. After 1858 Leeds fattened and grew a little smug. It never really grew beautiful, as if the struggle had been in vain.

In this chapter, we look at the development of a polite side of Leeds, in the persona of Headingley, for many years its richest residential quarter and its alternative to the tree-lined city squares which were never properly completed. Headingley substitutes for the elegance of Woodhouse Square, Hannover Square and Queen's Square, each of which was to be in some measures the imitation of Park Square. In each case, however, the four sides of the square were completed piecemeal and in different idioms. In Headingley, we can see a business and professional community detached from the city centre. The consequences to Leeds have been longlasting.

For world-wide radio audiences, Headingley is a sloping pitch and a batsman's wicket. There must be hundreds of thousands of devoted cricket fans scattered over the continents of the earth who purse their lips thoughtfully at mere mention of 'the Kirstall Lane end' who could hardly place Leeds itself on a map of England. As a shrine to cricket Headingley is indeed something special, uniting the West Indian cane-cutter and the Australian fence-rider in holy communion.

The Headingley ground as well as being a Test venue (for Yorkshiremen, *the* Test venue) is also the home of that most enigmatic of institutions, Yorkshire County Cricket Club. Cricket in Yorkshire is a barn-door target for any writer, in part religion, part poetry, part myth—rather like the Old Testament in fact. Headingley's possession of this famous ground offers the place an additional enjoyment much beloved by Yorkshiremen, an opportunity for the tail to wag the dog. There is something irresistible in this for Yorkshire folk and Headingley makes the most of it. Here is a postal sub-district of a large city with more real fame than all the rest put together, according to its lights.

So where *is* Headingley? It started life as little more than a dusty country crossroads, a long, winding hill away from Leeds. Under a particularly flourishing oak tree the ancient wapentake (or local parliament) of Skyrack and Morley met, and it is from this original oak that the pub close to the cricket ground takes its name. The oak was thought by Thoresby to date from Druidic times and was not finally removed until 1941, when it was a vast trunk, more like a piece of sculpture than a site for alfresco parliamentary proceedings. The tree certainly pre-dated Kirkstall Abbey.

Headingley fell outside the early manor of Leeds and only came into the parish of Leeds later on. We can get some idea of its growth from a very short account of the history of its church. Three churches have been built upon the site of St. Michael's, which is exactly opposite the original oak, the earliest building dating from 1627. This is a comparatively late date, and it is interesting that the land itself was given by Sir John Savile in 1619. His gift to Leeds was the heraldic arms embodied on its coat-of-arms. Savile lands abounded round Leeds, Savile becoming in time Baron of Pontefract and his son Earl of Sussex. (The second Earl of Sussex died without issue and the grand-daughter of Sir John inherited. She married Lord Brudenell, and their son became Earl of Cardigan. It was Cardigan land that was sold off to make the Test ground in 1888.)

This first church was properly a chapel in the parish of Leeds. It was helped into existence by gifts from a devout farmer, Mr. James Cotes. Its congregation was never very large and its importance qualified by its position. In those days, Headingley was over the hill from Leeds with a vengeance. It was usually lumped in with its lowly neighbour Burley, below Kirkstall on the banks of the Aire. Headingley was simply another untidy hamlet on a hill.

In 1837, however, the old church was demolished and a larger more spacious building erected on the same site. Now things were beginning to happen in the world at large, things in which Headingley had its part to play. The architect of the new church was Chantrell, who went on to rebuild Leeds Parish Church, as we have seen. Chantrell's St. Michael's was set in a community which had now grown to about 1,800 souls. It was the Archbishop of York's stipulation that the church should seat 600 of them.

Even in an age noted for its sabbatarian pieties, it is really remarkable that only forty years after, this second church was found to be too small. Even with the consecration in 1869 of St. Chad's, Far Headingley, the congregation of St. Michael's found its pews overcrowded and its services packed out to the doors. It closed for a year to make interior alterations, but in 1875 a congregational meeting resolved to look around for a larger site. The scene was set for a first-class ecclesiastical row.

The 'gentlemen of the committee' were part of a new, influential congregation. Their subscription list raised £2,000 almost immediately and they set about their quarrel with the clergy with a good deal of business acumen. For Headingley had now become just far enough from Leeds to find favour as an elevated, healthy suburb. Just as Burley had grown in a steady red pulse of cheap housing, Headingley had built from local Potternewton stone the houses of the rich. The mark of Victorian elegance is in these houses, plaster ceilings, tiled passages, bell pushers for the maid, stabling for the carriage. The new gentry had found Headingley and found it wholesome.

The committee first fell out with their own vicar, Henry Tuckwell, a former chaplain to the Leeds prison. It was found that enlargement of the church could not be made without displacement of some of the graves. Tuckwell threatened to resign if this happened. The laity then considered a site for an additional chapel of ease, to be put on the corner of Shaw Lane and the Otley Road. This was delicate thinking, for the land actually fell into the neighbouring parish, but the Vicar of St. Chad's reluctantly agreed.

Dr. Gott, the Vicar of Leeds, was required to give his consent to this new arrangement. He refused. We can get something of the temper of these 'gentlemen of the committee' from their final bitter, lashing report to the members of the church: "The hinderers have triumphed and the church suffers, but the solemn responsibility attendant on that inglorious victory must rest, not as the avowed enemies of the Church of England, but with the Vicar of Leeds and his open or secret abettors."

This is the indignant tone of the man who sends for the head-waiter, demands to see the manager, knocks down the black-guard with a straight left, or, significantly, goes out in appalling light to bat against demon bowling. It is the voice of wealth, command, and confidence.

The rebuilding of St. Michael's was taken up again in 1881, this time by the new vicar, Frederick John Wood. Wood was prepared to move grave sites to accomplish his task; again Headingley was plunged into complete uproar, this time from those who did not hesitate to accuse Wood of grave-robbing, or to claim that opening up the graves would lead to wide-scale plague. Poor Wood. Characterized in letters and pamphlets as a 'Romanizer', urged on by one party to rebuild the church, and warned by another that only the Archangel Gabriel had rights of removal over the sleeping dead! It took a diocesan court, counsel for both sides, submissions to the Archbishop of York, and endless paper before the present church was consecrated on Thursday 8th July 1886. Four years late the bishop gratefully lowered the highest stone in the steeple in to its place (by means of a pulley and rope reaching to the ground). The applause was gentlemanly and restrained.

There are several interesting points about this story. The first is the obvious one, that what was a small, devout community of farmers in 1619 had grown into a complex suburban congregation, but one in which the authority of wealth predominated. Yet although Headingley may have wished for the greatest independence possible within the city, it was plucked back from its most ardent dreams quite easily. The men who grew to dislike Gott so fervently were the new middle class of Leeds, the settled sediment of the great tidal expansion of the century's wealth.

There is something very characteristic in this curious story, not least the way in which the quarrels reveal a desire to be settled, to make a solid respectable worthy life in Leeds. The realization the congregation of St. Michael's at last acknowledged was that Headingley *was* Leeds. Any permanent settlement would have to include that admission.

In the twentieth century, Headingley presents a curious mixture of styles and possibilities. The big houses are still there and the quiet streets still echo to the footfall as they did in the heyday of controversy. But the Otley Road, which was once the hill that led away to Leeds in one direction and the Wharfe in the other, has become a commuter artery. It pours traffic clean through the old Headingley—what there is of it that is left. There are plans for a by-pass and plans for turning at least some of the district back to village pace by the making of pedestrian precincts. These plans are like the staunching of a mortal wound.

The private developers have had their try at surgery. Headingley now has its own urban centre, a large block of shops with a defunct bowling alley at one end. The development was not enormously popular in the area and has not solved all the problems the district faces. Headingley is rather like Hampstead in character, putting forward the strongest argument for the place. A great many students live there in lodgings and halls of residence. So do many members of the university and polytechnic. Every city needs its Hampstead, perhaps, if only to make possible entertainment and recreation for the sort of people who like to eat out or watch foreign films, or buy handmade pottery, or whatever. It would be nice to report that Headingley provides these things for and on behalf of the city as a whole. It doesn't. The best thing still that Headingley can offer is grass—the famous cricket table, back to back with the only underground-heated Rugby League pitch in Yorkshire.

Cricket at Headingley is one of the summertime pleasures the city has to offer and on the occasion of a Test Match Leeds plays host to its traditional rivals in Yorkshire. Men from Bradford, Huddersfield, Sheffield—men who might normally speak of Leeds with, let us say, some reserve in their voice are pleased to come to Headingley.

The game is one of the reinforcing strands of the great Yorkshire myth. It fits a Yorkshireman like a well-cut suit of clothes and a championship game at Headingley, or a Test, is one of the festival occasions when a Leeds man assumes his other citizenship as a Yorkie. Cricket stands to Yorkshire as rugby football does to the Rhondda: it is something that has gone deeper than any analysis or joke can touch. The great supremacy the county had in the 'thirties may account for some of the enthusiasm for the game. In those far-off sunlit afternoons Yorkshire pride was surfeited time and again by great championship cricket. But there is more.

Cricket pre-dates almost all of contemporary Leeds. They were betting on the game when Leeds was just another market-town. As Leeds grew, we have seen how it grew away from its background. It grew less and less like the county of rolling acres, not more like it. But no one can ever forfeit his Yorkshire citizenship in Yorkshire. Wherever you are born, you are a Yorkshireman first and always. This is as true of Leeds as anywhere else. One or two things help bind the emotional knot between the hill farmer and the Leeds clerk, the deep-sea fisherman out of Hull and the Leeds 'bus conductor. One of them is undoubtedly cricket.

An incomer often finds this difficult to grasp. Intense rivalries do exist in Yorkshire and patriotism can be very local indeed, sometimes contracted to a single street, as we shall see. But when it comes to the rest of the country, a greater patriotism takes sway. That spirit is almost the spirit of nationalism itself. Cricket helps along that greater loyalty. In recent times when Close and Illingworth captained the Test side, the popular idea of the English team in any Leeds pub was that of a bunch of raw lads with lah-di-dah ways who needed knocking into shape. "A strong Yorkshire means a strong England" is no idle motto. It is more in the nature of a national anthem.

Because Leeds is the home of the county side, it has its full share of this national emotion. There are few if any parallels elsewhere in the country. London does not feel a special sentiment for any one of the Home Counties, neither does Birmingham take out citizenship in Warwickshire. Yet in any situation at all in Leeds, it will be unusual if a man does not sooner or later talk about himself as a Yorkshireman as well as a Loiner. He knows very well that when he goes abroad—in other words, when he crosses the Don—he will have to defend not just his home town, but his whole county. When he's casting around for things of excellence to boast of, cricket is there and to hand. And who has not heard of Headingley?

Leeds is an example of a city without great aristocratic patronage. Headingley, in its guise as a cricket headquarters, is one of the few places where 'county' Yorkshire meets industrial Yorkshire. The Yorkshire County Cricket Club itself is an amalgam of those two interests and the same wedding of personality has taken the field at Headingley for nearly 100 years. In men like

Freddie Trueman, Willie Wardle, Brian Close, Ray Illingworth, there is a direct and immediate identification by all of Leeds' working population. These men are the dour, grafting, dogged sort of characters Leeds understands very well. Part of the fun of cricket in Yorkshire has been to see them play off their character against the side's great amateurs, and the gentlemen of the county committee.

Freddie Trueman was once described by Harold Wilson of Huddersfield as "the greatest living Yorkshireman". When Mr. Wilson became Prime Minister in 1964, our Freddie sent him a cable saying, with just the right amount of laconic wit, "Welcome to the Club". Trueman was a collier at Maltby Main when he was discovered by Yorkshire. He epitomizes the Yorkshireman struggling to escape from every Leeds man—cocky, tough, dedicated, wonderfully direct. For the rest of his life he will be 'our Freddie' to men who have never played cricket in their life, never been down a pit and never lost their way and landed up at the gates of Maltby Main.

Leeds and Yorkshire join hands at Headingley. The gentry are brought face to face with the industrial worker. Nothing else could do that in quite that way. For the rest of the year it is Leeds United and the Yorkshire Show, Leeds Rugby League and the Harrogate Festival—in other words, difference. At Headingley the difference is sunk. For many who live in Leeds, there is no other reason to visit Headingley, and many who come in by car to Headingley from far afield know the quiet streets round about the ground rather better than they know the city centre. Headingley has therefore the dubious honour of being a special kind of meeting ground for much more than cricket itself. When the crowds have settled in appreciative silence round the sacred table of grass, something is happening in Leeds that could not happen anywhere else. The city is shaking hands, cautiously and guardedly. with its long-lost relative, the county gentry.

There is a story which illustrates all this and relates the game to the people who watch it. It is told by the novelist John Braine. Braine and Sir Leonard Hutton were both guests at a *Yorkshire Post* literary luncheon. It was at the height of Braine's success as the author of *Room at the Top*. Sir Leonard offered to drive him home, which he did with great dash and it seemed to Braine, very slightly the worse for wear after an excellent lunch. "I thought all the time of that night's headlines in the *Yorkshire Evening Post*," Braine said afterwards. "Sir Leonard Hutton and other man killed in car crash."

VII

HUNSLET

A CONTRAST in Leeds is raw and unsubtle stuff. If a thing is not one thing, it is another. There is little gradation of tone, or dubiety in deciding what is what.

Only a couple of miles from the quiet, wealth and dignity of Headingley is Hunslet. You may 'reside' in Headingley; in Hunslet you occupy a dwelling. There are plenty of Headingley residents who if they were set down in parts of Hunslet would hardly know which county they were in, let alone which city. In Headingley, every inch of space is used to some good purpose. In Hunslet, no-man, that mysterious tenant, has his land alongside many a street. No-man's land only occurs in the Hunslets of our cities.

In the language of public apology, this is industrial Leeds. You can excuse Hunslet by pointing to Leeds' wealth. After all, in the next parish, still inside the city boundary, is a colliery. Running through the district is one of the earliest railways from that pit to the city proper. In the next parish is a power-station and a steel works. Between the river and the city boundary are, what, a hundred factories and works? You don't get brass without muck, and Hunslet pays the price of Leeds' wealth. It is hard, this land-scape, and cruel: a good many gates and fences, padlocks and bars, warning signs and guard dogs. It is a flat, broken-nosed kind of landscape, wearing the face of a tough, phlegmatic man. No masters live in Hunslet. It is a place for the men.

Nothing sums up Hunslet so much as Parkside, home of an honoured Rugby League side. They play Rugby League at Headingley, of course—and spin money from it. Headingley is Leeds' ground—a great side, a winning side, a cup-holding glamour side. League at Headingley is a sporting occasion in the modern idiom—excitement, success and championships. It is a

mild Saturday in January. Hunslet are entertaining Featherstone
Rovers, while Leeds play Wigan at Headingley.

The total gate for the Parkside game would fit comfortably
into a part of the Headingley terraces. The way to the ground is
across the tracks of the old Middleton railway. It is a pleasant
stroll (down a muddy lane) in the company of short, quiet men.
Donkeys are quartered on one side of the track. On the other,
in a deep pit of rubbish the skeleton of a Leeds tram weathers
forlornly. If a film director like Lindsay Anderson were to choose
an evocation of sadness in the heart of a bustling city, he could
not arrange a better locale. It is like walking into a novel by Stan
Barstow, this unhurried walk to the Parkside ground. The air
is quiet and still.

The ground is fenced off with a very tall fence, served by four
turnstiles. A man exclaims in surprise, "Nay, a bloody queue now.
They'll be having policemen on white horses next." About ten
people have formed the queue. They all turn round to laugh and
shake their fists at the man walking up towards them.

In fact there are altogether two policemen in the ground, and
about 500 fans. Under the stands there are two licensed bars, with
faded photographs of the 1954 season (including a photograph of
Miss Marjorie Ramsey, Hunslet Queen for that year).

Parkside is a very good, very green pitch. The main stand looks
down the pitch to a small bank at the far end, and behind that a
slag heap. The club offices and team rooms are in a ramshackle
wooden building painted green. The member's stand is beside it,
with seats held by the illustrious, the men dignified by civic
duties, the forgotten and the humble. You pay your five bob for
the ground and only another shilling for the seated stand.

Everything about Hunslet R.L.F.C. has a family feel. Because
the crowds that used to flock here have gone away, it does not
mean that the spirit of the club has vanished with them. On the
contrary. The mood is something between a church social and a
work's outing. The pleasant smiles and friendly service are
unforced and apparently commonplace. The bars empty at
precisely thirty seconds to kick-off, and the fans walk up in the
terraces with something of a sense of belonging.

Rugby League is a game that has unusual problems. Although
television has done a good deal to help some sports—for example

show jumping, swimming and motocross, it has had, by general agreement among the clubs, a disastrous effect upon the major part of Rugby League. Live coverage of Rugby League matches has greatly enhanced the popularity of the game in the South, while drastically reducing the gates. Although watching moto-cross might make you long for a motor bike, watching a team game on television does not make you want to get up and go to the ground next week. The crowds for Rugby League were never colossal; but television has drastically reduced them. In the case of the smaller clubs, it has had a crippling effect.

This is in spite of the hand-out received by the clubs as their share of broadcasting rights. The great post-war sides of the league game can compete with soccer, although on disfavourable terms, since very few soccer matches are televised as they happen. Top class league sides gain publicity for their class players by television exposure. Smaller clubs—and losing sides—stand to gain nothing but kicks. The ha'pence from television is offset by falling gates and divided fan loyalties.

Hunslet is in the latter position. For five years past it has been a small, rundown club without much playing success in a district which has been rapidly depopulated by major rehousing schemes. On the other side of the main road, less than a mile away, the star of Leeds United has risen to eclipse almost everything else in sight. The club at first refused to join in the television presentation of football at its ground. When it was forced to, for the sake of the fee-share-out, it was too late to benefit. When a new scheme of payments to players was introduced, the Hunslet directors were forced into unhappy dispute with their staff. The club was literally starving to death.

Hunslet players are probably among the lowest paid in the whole league. They are on £7 a match, £12 if they win. The money is so ridiculously low by comparison with footballer's wages that it is almost risible. Something other than money makes a professional sportsman, obviously: but the Hunslet lads must be especially dedicated. Of the team fielded against Featherstone, all but three are local lads. Of the thirteen players, ten are under twenty-one.

They play to the sort of round abuse only a family can exercise, the most stick coming from the women. Hunslet scores four tries

to Featherstone's three, but their place kicking is appalling and
they throw their £5 win-bonus away, not once but three or four
times. They produce the sort of finish that often comes in rugby
league, with a sudden switch of fortunes that lifts the 600-strong
crowd to its toes. The home side loses by a couple of points and
walks off dejectedly. Apart from the missed chances, they have
been truly unlucky to lose.

The club was founded in 1891 at a meeting attended by 500
local men. In its eighty years of existence it has been to Wembley
twice. It won the Challenge Trophy in 1934 and was beaten
finalist in 1965. In that '65 team were names that are still current in
much grander teams today. Almost before the Wembley roar
faded the club was forced to sell. Geoff Gunney, probably the
greatest player the club ever had, remained as the team coach. He
was awarded the M.B.E. for his services to the game.

In 1907-8, the Golden Season, Hunslet won all four major
trophies and in 1938 a crowd of 52,000 cheered them home in the
Challenge Cup against rivals Leeds, at Elland Road, home of
Leeds United. All that excitement and glamour has faded away
now. The net profit from a game today may be as low as £60 and
the club is in the unenviable situation of having a valuable freehold
which it uses for ninety minutes every other Saturday. In present-
day economic terms, Parkside is a disaster area.

It is all the more pity that it is such an attractive proposition as a
sporting venue. Without the overcrowding and discomfort of
Elland Road, but without the great playing success of its closest
neighbour Leeds R.L.F.C., the Parkside is trapped by circumstances. It would be a popular venue if the team suddenly hit a
winning streak. But even if they performed the impossible and
won at Wembley, they would be forced into selling players to
recoup their finances. The cycle would start all over again.

The continentals have solved this problem by building super-
stadia in which all sports can be accommodated. (In Gothenburg,
for example, which is a Swedish port-city much smaller than
Leeds, there is already one beautifully appointed football ground
and a second in the building.) Real Madrid is probably the best
known of these super-stadia and the Aztec stadium in Mexico the
most recent. But would this solution satisfy Parkside, Hunslet?

The Northern Rugby Union was densely concentrated in

Yorkshire. It depended for its survival upon primarily local support. In the way cities have turned out, local is an adjective which has been stretched a point or two. In Hunslet it still means what it says. Parkside's honourable existence has been supported by men who have lived only a few streets away. At most the traditional support came from no more than a mile to see the match. When the worst of Hunslet was destroyed for the best of reasons, some of the best went with it.

By an Act of 1758 Charles Brandling was granted rights to build a wagon-way from his pit in Middleton to the Aire. He undertook to deliver the city 23,000 tons of coal annually at the fixed price of 4s. 8³/₁₀d. per ton. What is more, the agreement had a term of sixty years. The Middleton railed-way was the earliest in the country.

In the days of steam traction, Hunslet became famous for engine-building, and the spin-off from heavy engineering techniques gave rise to smaller workshops and more complex industrial growth in the area. There was no legislation to deal with forward planning of city growth until the Town Planning Act of 1909. Up to that time industrial advantage and human habitation mixed inextricably in Hunslet. Houses were built up to the gates of factories, claypits sunk behind those houses, yards and depots fenced off in the handiest place without much regard to residential amenity.

Unlike some areas of Leeds, where the housing followed the banks of a beck, filled the valley and that was that, Hunslet has shifted uneasily, creaking and groaning with the stress of industrialization. It is the part of Leeds that has been the last to be flooded with cheap housing and among the last to be cleared. Girls went out of Hunslet to tailor or to serve in shops. The men stayed to work in the heavy industry or to join the small master in his workshop. In their heyday, the smell in the streets was of machine oil and the population was cheek-by-jowl with its place of work. The staple unit of measurement was a street.

The present Director-General of UNESCO comes from Hunslet. Richard Hoggart's book about working-class attitudes and their confrontation with the mass-media was first published in 1957. *The Uses of Literacy* was the first full account of post-war working-class values and gained much of its immediate success

Kirkstall Abbey

for its personal, autobiographical content. Hoggart's Hunslet
has been the subject of study in schools and colleges all over the
country. He himself was of a kind that Britain had begun to
produce in great quantity—first generation graduates with inborn
working-class backgrounds who were forced to review their own
personal history as part of their process of education. The book
struck a chord with many hundreds of teachers and university
staff lecturers who were attracted by its integrity and exactness
of description. The degree of self-consciousness Hoggart was
able to employ in his vivid description of Hunslet was matched
before long by others, some of them only from a few streets
away in the same locality.

The novelist Keith Waterhouse and the playwright Willis
Hall were born in Hunslet. So was the actor Peter O'Toole. At
the end of the 'fifties there was a sudden surge of new writing
about the industrial North of England. In addition to the men
already mentioned, Stan Barstow in Ossett, David Storey in
Wakefield and John Braine in Bingley were all at work. All of
them worked independently of each other, but each from
roughly the same starting point. By comparison with their
literary predecessors of the 'thirties, the new generation wrote
directly from experience. They were not observers but partici-
pants. Their work was intensely subjective but painfully honest.
Like Hoggart's pioneering book, they made what had been mere
local colour to previous writers into a complex whole, with its
own meanings and values, its own life.

Hoggart drew particular attention to one aspect of life in
Hunslet. His grandparents were pulled into the city from a rural
childhood. He was the child of the streets. For Hoggart himself,
the streets were his landscape, his whole environment. It left in
him a profound sense of locality, and a feeling for the physical
immediacy of a working-class environment which he describes
with startling accuracy. The 'local', 'a local lad', 'she lives local',
is part of the common reference in all urban working-class
districts: the adjective is always an exact description. The streets
interconnect in a pattern that cannot be understood by driving
round them in a car. The street is the way to measure much more
than mere distance. The street is the natural extension of the
hearth.

7

The Parkinson Building looms over the last of Beech Grove

The loss of the street and its culture in major rehousing projects is unavoidable but disastrous. The new Hunslet embodied in the Leek Street development is a poor substitute for what was. Leeds has a slum clearance programme that has been the envy of many other cities in Britain. The problem has not been one of land but financial capacity. In Hunslet, as the old slums have gone down under the bulldozer, the way has been made clear for the first really comprehensive plan for industry and housing in that area of the city since the district was first developed. Until the population was rehoused, the city authorities had little power over the most of their problems. The people had to come first.

Hunslet Grange is a housing project which will accommodate over 3,000 people. The unit cost of housing has of course risen to astronomic proportions. Leek Street is the best available solution, but it is not the best solution by a long way. If there are immediate gains to the tenants, these are offset by losses that are not less important by being less tangible. In time Hunslet will be 'developed' to the capacity of the city's spending power. With the population out of the way, the industry can be tackled and the area redrawn in the spirit of the 'seventies and 'eighties of this century. Part of the anxiety always at the back of the city's mind is the fear for the recession of Leeds's dominance as an area of mixed economy. As a regional city, which it is now, Leeds needs to keep all the balls in the air at once: rehousing, education, industrial regeneration, communications. Standing in the way, at all turns, is the legacy of nineteenth-century *laissez faire* economics.

As they have found out at Parkside, Hunslet has changed since 1957 when Richard Hoggart put it on the map in such an emphatic way. The demands of 'the mass' have expressed themselves in a harsh form. The sort of uniformity and invitation to conform that Hoggart identified in the candy-floss world of the mass-media have their parallel in political and economic reasoning. Leeds is highly regarded in the pecking-order of local authorities in England and Wales. Its chairman of council, Sir Frank Marshall, is also chairman of the national association of local authorities and one of the leading figures of English local government. Sir Frank's problems of city-management are of a scale and importance that would tax many junior Ministers of State. In that scheme of things, the redevelopment of Hunslet poses a special problem.

As Hoggart himself pointed out, it is all too easy to sentimentalize Hunslet. It is no solution to slum housing to speak instead of the wonderful characters or warm-hearted decencies thrown up by impoverished conditions. At the same time, a community cannot be planned on a drawing board. When one is taken away, another does not spring up in its place. It will take many years before Leek Street is anything more than a forbidding barracks. It seems all the more pity that in one small area, Hunslet Parkside, which is such good value for money, the community is losing its heartsblood. In fact, the whole of the old Hunslet is bleeding to death.

No city can tolerate the sort of housing for which Leeds was infamous in the last century. The health and safe keeping of Leeds depends on a solution to the problems of Hunslet. That solution has, in the nature of the problems it faces, to be sweeping and comprehensive. In the clean-slate redevelopment Leeds is committed to, some of its actual heritage will disappear. It will need more than a slogan to replace that. The motorway city of the 'seventies will need to be more than a noisy cross roads if it is to be a tolerable place in which to live. There are some qualities in life that you cannot put on wheels, and some energies more precious than petrol or jet fuel.

VIII

HOMES FOR TWO HUNDRED THOUSAND

HEADINGLEY and Hunslet are not the only vivid contrast to be found in Leeds but they do help us to a view of Leeds that reflects an old nineteenth-century pattern. On the one hand the master's lofty suburb, on the other the flat and dismal plain, where plainness predominates: it is the sort of comparison which Mrs. Gaskell sought when she came to Manchester. Smaller West Riding towns still show this division of interests and loyalties. You can find your way to a meeting hall or a new school or the house of a solicitor or doctor by following the pattern of house styles. The two districts we have reviewed formed many a smaller town. All over the West Riding when an industrial community has gathered by a river, the waste and the squalor is at the centre and the privacy and wealth up on the hills. You quickly get a feel for locality and the possibilities it contains. It is no great exaggeration to say that a perceptive eye can judge to a street where to find, for example, a washateria, a cinema, a second-hand shop, a sub-station of the police, or a delicatessen.

Leeds is far larger and proportionately more complex. Up to the end of the First World War there was a desperate kind of uniformity about its housing, for no fewer than 70,000 back-to-back houses had been flung up to meet the explosion of population. Back-to-back houses were no anachronistic hangover from the bad old days either. Between 1874 and 1909 12,000 of them were built. As greater control could be exercised over private building and land-acquisition, and as the general expectation of what constituted a reasonable living standard rose, this housing became an intolerable burden on the city. No more were built, and those that were up earliest came down first.

The whole of Yorkshire suffers chronically from bad housing. The Yorkshire and Humberside Economic Planning Council reviewed the region in 1966. In the paragraphs of the review which dealt with sub-standard housing, the council took as its lowest estimate the figure for 'statutory' unfitness, which is based on standards set out in the Housing Act of 1957. It then took an expert estimate of those houses with a rateable value of less than £30 per annum. Such houses are most likely to have been built before 1914 and to be deficient in most of the amenities we would consider proper to decent tenancy. The lowest figure which resulted was 138,000 and the highest 522,000. The council urged the higher figure as the more realistic. Included in those half-million houses were 298,000 without hot water, 377,544 without a fixed bath and 213,381 without a w.c. These figures derive from the 1961 census. They are a national scandal.

The figures startled Yorkshire when they were published. They are an antidote to the sentimental affection in which the York-shireman holds his townscapes—and they reveal incidentally the comparatively low level of standards to be found in the statutory definition of unfitness of the 1957 Act. They are the statistical evidence of a problem that is extremely hard to combat. Housing in Britain is still a local responsibility. For the poorer housing authorities simply to bring their housing stock to tolerable standard is an almost superhuman task. The will to change things is not enough. To bring the region's housing up to standard would cost well over £1,000 million, reckoning the unit cost of a dwelling as no more than £2,000. It is a sum that national government finds it convenient to forget. It is not to be wondered that in the small housing authorities there is despair.

The task in Leeds was made apparent much earlier than 1965 and it did not need an economic review to bring the worst to light. As we have seen, Leeds housing of the 1830–40 period was a scandal as it was being built. It did not take many years for the whole inner city to be choked by housing which met few if any of the requirements we would now consider to be the basic rights of a human being. Leeds housing was bad housing. Only full employment and steady wages kept the lid on a situation which out-of-work and starving tenants would have reduced to a disaster.

The city is the third largest in area of any outside London. Its commercial and industrial prosperity—and in particular its mixed

economy which kept it going through bad patches of its growth—
also gave it the means to do something about its housing problems. It started late in redevelopment, but no later than anywhere
else. It had the essential prerequisites for the job—high ratable
values and plenty of space. It did not have the sort of statutory
powers or financial backing the whole nation has lacked for so
long, but it did what it could with the tools that it had. In this
light Leeds has some reason to be proud of its efforts. Its critics—
especially its younger generation—might reflect. Under the system
as it was and is, Leeds has done a more than creditable job. The
system may be wrong but you cannot blame Leeds for that.

Before the war there were 21,700 municipal tenancies. A
further 41,000 have been added since the war ended. At the
present time the rate of growth is in the order of 1,500 a year and
there are in addition 7,219 residential properties acquired by the
council but not built by them. This total provides accommodation
for over 200,000 people and as we shall see the greater part of this
population has found a new roof over its head and a more
equitable rent in the last thirty-five years. Leeds housing has
undergone a quiet revolution well within the lifetime of the
greater part of its working people. The revolution has been a
quiet one only because other people's houses have no great
publicity value unless they are bigger than the one you live in
yourself. But if one adds in the revolution in education, health and
welfare that such a massive redeployment of housing entails, we
can see something of the colossal significance this has had upon
Leeds as a city.

The beginnings of the Leeds slum clearance programme are in
the period 1934–39. The terrible housing to the east of the markets,
where once the railway had its terminus, the York Road, and
parts of Burmantoft was demolished and new estates created at
opposite ends of the city, in Middleton and Gipton. In the centre
of this massive redevelopment, which affected 30,000 houses
before it ended, the council created Quarry Hill Flats. For years
this was the most famous landmark in the city, for its concept
was revolutionary.

Quarry Hill Flats are built on twenty-three acres of land at the
eastern end of the Headrow. The space they occupy is about a
third of the total acreage of Leeds when Bischoff, Hall, Beckett

and Priestley were the leaders of the community. But of the total area, only 18 per cent is built upon. The flats range from four to eight storeys high and comprise 938 separate units. Quarry Hill was one of the first high-rise, high-density housing estates to attempt a solution to the problem of community. Built into the development was, as best the architects could devise, a sense of locality. The design, which is now a commonplace, tries to curl its housing round an open precinct and 'lung' to the concrete and glass. Quarry Hill was provided with its own shops, its own privacy and an opportunity to 'be somewhere', rather than being simply a place to store people when they must eat and sleep.

The development was not entirely without the woolly idealism that touched so much of the 'thirties. Quarry Hill is an unprotected site round the outside curve of its length. A bus station is opposite and the road is heavy with traffic at all times. New York Road, the only city-centre exit to the east runs past its northern wall. The flats are close by the main shopping area and the markets, but they lack the sort of concession to individuality, crankiness and eccentricity that makes communities cling together. In the 'thirties when concrete and glass were exciting words in the mouths of Marxist poets, and the urban proletariat was thought to be in need of nothing more than a bicycle, a rucksack and a copy of *Penguin New Writing* to make life complete, Quarry Hill was a marvel.

In the 1960s Leeds tried to repeat its success with Quarry Hill on a new site to the extreme east of the city, in the outlying villages of Seacroft, Whinmoor and Swarcliffe. There a new population of some 85,000 people was housed in high-rise tower blocks mixed with low-density development. Seacroft, which has come to be the name used for the whole area, has more people in it than some completely independent townships. It is in a favoured site if private building is anything to go by, for next round the ring-road to it are Roundhay, Moortown and Alwoodley, which are the sites of post-war private speculation. With a population of this size, Seacroft is a community willy-nilly, if only on the argument that you can hardly describe it otherwise.

This time, the planners centred the development up with the sort of provision a new town of this size could not do without.

Incorporated in the municipal plan was a town centre which includes four multiple stores, seventy shops and an open-air market. There is a library, a post office, a clinic and six banks. To the east of the ring road the new town has its own industrial estate.

We can see from city plans that Seacroft hardly existed before 1940, except in a small area round its village green and at its southern boundary with Cross Gates, which is on the Leeds–York railway line. Into these empty spaces which led gently away to far-off forgotten hamlets like Ledsham, which shares its place-name with Leeds and is as old, the municipality have constructed a suburb of its own that is likely to prove a test-case for urban renewal in the whole region.

Her Majesty the Queen opened Seacroft in 1965 when the putty in the windows was hardly dry. In its six years of life, Seacroft has struggled to come alive as a limb of Leeds. The problems it faces are almost as great as the problems it solved. Like many Greater London housing schemes Seacroft is so big that it could easily be the tail to wag the dog. But like them, it is populated by people with an affectionate memory for another place altogether. Seacroft has all the potential support a Rugby League side could want, but no Hunslet Parkside with its strong tea and fading photographs of past glories. In other words, it is still a child.

One of the difficulties Seacroft shares with its predecessor Quarry Hill is this. It is almost impossible for a plan to have a significant factor of the unpredictable, or chance occurrence. After all, that is what planning is *for*, the planners can object: a plan is not a plan if you are not sure what will happen to part of it. This problem is crucial to new communities. You cannot provide everything 80,000 people will need by an architectural plan. Even if you include in your plan social amenities such as you think will be popular, or encourage them after the building is complete, you cannot be sure they will flourish. The reason for this is obvious. Human problems are problems of human relationships. Human relationships are not determined solely by architecture. A good architectural environment can suggest possibilities and release new energies; it cannot *solve* anything.

The community of Seacroft has not had a particularly good press. People who have never been inside a council estate in their life have been quick to complain about vandalism, tenant apathy or tenant belligerence. Moreover, Seacroft is a barn-door target for its new population. It would be extremely unusual if there were not trouble from all sides and the more trouble there is, the more likelihood of community growth, if the disputes are faced head-on by their solutions. One can perhaps take a simple example to describe the whole.

One of the problems all housing estates have is with their young. Council tenancies are predicated on a family size of 2·9 persons. This is the statistical average of family size for the region. You do not need to be a statistician to grasp that the nine-tenths of your total family represented by a mess of football boots, crash helmets, Jimi Hendrix posters, undone homework, dirty socks and chewing gum wrappers is averse to joining yourself and your other whole unit of family size for a quiet stroll round a street identical to your own. Families need to live together under the same roof: after that simple moral precept, all hell breaks loose. They often do not eat together; they go out at different times in morning, come home at different hours at night. They dress differently, have different entertainment, different sorts of outside relationships. Only in television advertisements do we see the entire 2·9 disporting itself on a lawn, or slurping down a hearty cereal breakfast, or kissing each other goodnight with a mug of steaming coloured milk. In other words, although the houses may be patterned the lives inside them are not. The family is a handy judicial and social unit of measure but it is not the only one.

The Hunslet Street or the Marsh Lane ginnel was not a lengthy, winding road but a short, compact, precise unit of community. So localized was the Leeds that has been pulled down that the University of Leeds Department of Dialect Studies has been able to confirm that there existed a quite separate accent for Hunslet and Woodhouse, although these areas were only a little over a mile apart.

In a crowded, badly ventilated back-to-back, it was natural for children and young people to play out of doors. As they grew older, the street itself became a part of their living-room. After dark, traffic was light and the streets empty. It was a safe enough environment—and it afforded complete privacy, if you knew where to go. Middle-class children at the same age are educated to consider the road and roadway as both dangerous and public. For them privacy is found at home, indoors. Out-of-doors is not their living-room, as it is with slum kids. There are special conventions for what you must wear and do out-of-doors.

Housing estates are laid according to middle-class concepts of dignity and their function is planned according to middle-class ideas of good usage. When the young of the new community are resettled, the change hits them the hardest. Without the real knowledge of what was bad about the old, they cannot be expected to go wild with enthusiasm for the new. An estate is not a street. You can feel no loyalty for an estate in quite the way you could for 'our lot' or 'Cider street kiddo's'. What in a slum was a group, on an estate is a gang. A penny scraped on edge into a soft red brick makes a beautiful round hole in time. In Hunslet, nobody scolds because brick is so common that people have stopped seeing it. In the same way the chalked slogans on the end wall, the goalposts painted up against the factory fence, the left-over white paint flung over the waste-ground fences.

But a single sapling snapped in two on an estate is enough to send the critics of Seacroft into paroxysms. In March Lane, you could sling a mattress down the back of an old car chassis and no-one would notice for a year. In new Seacroft you get the feeling that binolculars are watching the open spaces, just in case.

Besides the problems which would have befallen the whole of Leeds without Seacroft, these issues are trivial. It is part of the peculiar Englishness of English things that they loom so large in everyday public discussion. Leeds has no problems of the kind that Liverpool and Glasgow face in their urban renewal programme. By comparison with their cities—and London—the character of the young in Leeds might be considered even a little priggish and goody-goody. When 200,000 people are involved, the story of Leeds and its municipal rehousing schemes can be nothing but a success.

The most recent scheme is the 'Little London' project which rises above Meanwood Road. The site is sloping and has a spur of the inner ring road driving through it. Thousands of motorists go to work under the bridge carrying Camp Road, which was once notorious for its prostitutes and thieves. To one side the high-rise towers seem to have sprung up overnight almost. They overlook the scene of some desperate living, not only along Camp Road and by the Barracks, but in nearby North Street, where the sweatshop tailors used to be. Little London is an exhilarating redevelopment because its towers and the fast moving road beside it suggest speed and confidence in the future. The planning possibilities of the whole project, which will stretch to join hands with the university and Woodhouse Moor, are enormous. Little London will be one of the most comprehensive valley redevelopments in Leeds. It replaces street after street of back-to-backs.

At the very top of the plan, unknown to the planners, lives Norman Smithson, a writer who was born in Woodhouse and has lived there all his life. Norman Smithson was a journalist on the old *Yorkshire Evening News* and when that folded devoted himself entirely to writing. Few Northern writers have a better grasp of what an urban landscape means to the figures in it, and few can write with as much compassion about the ordinary events of life. Almost unknown in his own city, Norman Smithson has been a writer's writer for ten years or more, honoured by the BBC and the Arts Council, respected by his fellow authors all over the North of England. He, better than anyone, could tell the boys behind the drawing-boards what Little London will need to replace 'the rhubarb fields forever' of his childhood. He is an example of the best that the old city could produce. Perhaps somewhere in the scheduled properties of the same district now is a kid who will emulate Smithson's patience with his material and complete an equal number of plays, scripts, stories and novels whilst staring out from a sixth-floor window at the soft smudge of Halton Hill. For the health of the new Little London, it had better be so.

IX

IMMIGRANTS

ONE of the most influential minorities in Leeds is its Jewish population. The Jewish community in the city is the second largest outside London. Manchester comes before and Glasgow follows after. There are many towns and cities with longer experience of Anglo-Jewry—Hull is an example in the West Riding; but none can show as sudden and dramatic a history. Perhaps only in London itself, in the Mile End and Whitechapel, was the growth of a Jewish community as rapid. There, close to the docks, crowding into an already established area of settlement, many thousands of Russian and Polish Jews created at the turn of the century a community that has dispersed itself and its energies throughout the metropolis.

In a provincial community like Leeds, which is as we have seen founded on hard work and independence, the Jewish contribution is peculiarly strong and energetic. A good part of the much-honoured Leeds independence stems from its great background of nonconformity, which gave it a sense of realism and the impulse to self help at a time when the Establishment was weak or indifferent. Nonconformity includes in its practice a high regard for education and a love of organization. In the time when some leading citizens actually preferred not to have Parliamentary representation, arguing that a Member of Parliament got folk into a greater muddle than leaving them to their own devices, the debt of gratitude they owed in saying this was to the Dissenting churches, with their trust in voluntarism and remarkable organizational gifts. The arrival of the Jews in Leeds was for them a descent among men who knew only too well the value of independent self-improvement. This may have been a factor in their easy assimilation.

Jewish scholars have examined the street and trade directories of eighteenth-century Leeds to discover whether there were any Jews living in the town then. There were, but their numbers were very small. While their business influence may have been considerable, there were not enough of them to make the normal conditions of an orthodox life possible. We know, for example, that until the Earl of Cardigan sold off a plot of land in Gelderd Road there was no Jewish cemetery in Leeds. Up until that year, 1840, Jews were taken to Hull to be buried. In 1842 the first official Jewish marriage was celebrated, with all the observances required by Judaic law.

On 13th March 1881 something happened to change all this. In St. Petersburg, Tsar Alexander II was on his way through the streets when a bomb was thrown under the carriage. The vehicle shattered into pieces and the horses gutted, but the Tsar was miraculously unhurt. He stepped completely unscathed from the wreckage and began to reassure bystanders. The scene was a confused and hysterical one. In the confusion a man ran up with a second bomb and shouted, "It is too early to thank God!" This second explosion took place literally at the Tsar's feet. A leg was blown off, and the other one shattered to pulp. A great wound was blown in his stomach and the face lacerated. Alexander was carried, still conscious, into the Winter Palace where he died among the hastily gathered members of the Imperial family. His wife had been skating and came with the skates still in her hands to the deathbed.

No Jewish reader of this book will need telling that blame was almost instantly laid at the door of the Jews. None of the conspirators were Jews themselves but there followed a series of dreadful reprisals—not a bloodbath, although a regiment of cavalry rode from the Winter Palace that night with lances at the attack but a long slow history of repression and harassment, for which this assassination was ostensible excuse.

At the time of his death, Alexander II was Tsar of an Empire of great size and really fearful disorganization. The Russian Empire was a clumsy but highly volatile explosive chain of nationalities and minorities, waiting for a fuse to be lit. In this chain, the Jewish link was a specially forged one.

Under an ordinance of 23rd December 1791, Russian Jews were forced to live in what was called the Pale of Settlement—fourteen provinces to the south and west of the capital. Bessarabia was added to the list in 1813. Discrimination against the Jews by law was fairly strict. Jews were chosen for compulsory military service before other groups; they were denied access to certain occupations and professions. Their entry into education was qualified. In addition they lived under the constant duress of the most ignorant kind of anti-semitism, that of the illiterate but devout peasants of Mother Russia.

They were a very substantial minority in a population which was itself a hodge-podge of nationalities and languages. In Poland, which was then a part of the Empire, the census returns for 1859 show a population of 600,000 Jews in a total of 4,764,000 inhabitants. One in three—half a million—of the population of towns was Jewish. Despite this astonishing fact, Jews lived by grace and favour of the Church and State, and nothing was done to discourage the crudest kind of grass roots racial hatred. The Ashkenazim of Eastern Europe were by no means the rich, usurious merchants drawn by Marlowe and Shakespeare. They were small traders and trademen, people making their way as best they could.

The bedrock anti-semitism displayed in the Russian Empire is extremely hard for English people to grasp and has no parallel. The force of anti-semitic feeling could be argued away as an over-sensitive reaction on the part of a self-conscious people to events which in themselves were not especially serious. This argument would have more weight if we did not know from recent Russian news that discrimination against Jews and an unreasoned hatred of them is as common today as it was then. Jews in military service in the days of the Empire were specially selected for the most degrading duties. Their release from service was often a matter of doubt. Those they left behind in the villages and towns were subject themselves to a constant harassment all the more bitter to them for being ecumenically unwarranted. Hatred was irrational, racialist and pretty well imbibed with the mother's milk.

Alexander III acceded to the throne at the age of thirty-seven. He was a tall, shambling bearlike man. In the eyes of Victoria, he disgraced the idea of sovereignty with his crude diplomacy, violent temper and childlike displays of physical strength. (He had a passion for bending pokers and twisting dinner forks into knots, a habit that must have sent a shudder through the Osborne entourage.) His father had been assassinated only hours after agreeing to new reforms and had been known as the Tsar-Liberator. Under his reign Russian politicians had agonized over the question of whether or not to have some kind of constituent assembly. Alexander III made it quite clear that the Tsardom was to be as absolute as he could make it. There was to be no appeasement and no forgiveness.

From this dramatic moment spring the steady immigration and flight of Jews from Eastern Europe, which continued to this country until the Aliens Act of 1905. The pogroms were not concentrated in one place or at one time. There was immediate reprisal at Elizavetgrad, Kiev and Odessa, followed by outbreaks of violence in Warsaw and Balta, in Podolia. In 1886 Jews were expelled completely from Kiev. At the Passover in 1891 they were ordered to leave Moscow. In the summer months that followed the assassination 'temporary rules' had been set up to regulate the lives and livelihood of Jews. They were forbidden to live or hold property anywhere but in towns. Later on there were severe restrictions on the numbers to be admitted to secondary schools or universities. Jews were barred from the practice of law and to some extent medicine. Local voting rights were withdrawn (although the payment of local taxes was not). In 1894, a state monopoly of the sale of spirits removed from many Jews the only way left to them of making a living.

The Jewish presence in the Russias had never been secure. Only their own forbearance had made things tolerable. Now, squashed between an illiterate peasant anti-semitism and cultured Russia's age-long preoccupation with russification—national pride and racial integrity—the Jews shared the miserable existence of Russia's other problem minorities, among them the Latvians, Lithuanians and Armenians. Their options were extremely unattractive. They could stay and become enmeshed deeper and deeper in the chaos of an Empire tearing itself to pieces, or they could flee. Half a million fled.

Leeds Jewry is almost completely composed of the victims of these pogroms. Unlike Birmingham and Manchester which had established and longstanding congregations, Leeds received, over a period of twenty-four years, something like an additional 30,000 of population. All of them were at the end of a journey which had taken them across Europe to Rotterdam, bringing with them only the luggage of the ordinary traveller, with perhaps a sack of tools. Very few spoke anything like fluent English, very few had anyone anywhere in England who was a relative or friend. The cost of a passage from Rotterdam to Hull or Grimsby was under £1. There was no problem at the dock. The shipping companies had learned to expect them. They were herded on to the boats and told to wait. It was something they had learned to do patiently.

The Humber ports were especially popular because they gave the shortest route to Liverpool, and so to America. 'Through ticket' immigrants had to pass through Leeds, as a staging post *en route* to Manchester and the Liverpool Canal. Many came no further than Leeds. Here was the fifth biggest city in England with a variety of trades in which Jews were traditionally skilled and enabled by their religion to work at. Pressures in Leeds were perhaps less severe than in London and Manchester. A high proportion of those who came were men, and of these the great majority were young men under forty. Immigration officials were impressed by their general good health and confident bearing. They had come to make an opportunity for themselves.

The opportunity started at Leeds railway station. A Jewish friend tells the story of his father walking off the train from Grimsby and staring about him nervously. 'Crimps'—the spivs who battened on to the immigrants as each train arrived—were working through the station forecourt in a frenzy of noise and argument. A man rushes up to our new arrival and seizing his baggage tosses it on to a handcart. He is the self-appointed guide to the Leylands, where he knows all Jews will want to go first. "What's your name lad?" The man gives it slowly and clearly, as he has done all across the European continent; in Leeds the guide wrinkles his nose in disgust. But the unpronounceable syllables clearly begin with the letter T and from that hectic moment on the family becomes Teeman. The newly named Mr. Teeman runs down Boar Lane after his fast-disappearing luggage.

The Leylands have almost gone now. Most Leeds Jews can tell you about the quarter in the greatest detail, chiefly because

The New Lecture Theatres in Mathematician's Court, the University

this is where most of them started. It is one of the conditions of
Jewish life that the individuals are formed together in a community. The needs of a Jewish community are complex and they
interchange with the needs of a religious congregation. In London,
for example, there was already a community established in the
Mile End and Whitechapel areas. Close to the docks, supplied
with all the needs of Jewish life, this community had encouraged
gradual dispersion to other areas as this became feasible. From
1881 to 1905, Whitechapel received more and more new immigrants, very much faster than the community leaders could
manage to cope with. Whole networks of streets—for example
around Flower and Dean Street—became exclusively Jewish in
character and occupation. This crowding into a relatively small
area was not unimaginative or timid thinking but a necessary
joining together.

So it was with the Leylands. Jews from all over Russia and
Poland gathered together for their own benefit in some of the
worst and most-hated streets to have been flung together in the
nineteenth century. Where Jews are, Jews must go. We can see
how the new community was based on the old from the foundation of synagogues in Leeds. The first duty of a new immigrant
from City Station was to enquire in the teeming streets for
'Landsmen'—people from their old town or village. Synagogues
were founded from among these men, who were strangers to
each other but at any rate could share something, if no more than
a memory of a dusty summer. 'Marienpol', 'Vilna', the 'Polish',
'the Lithuanian' are all names of synagogues deriving from the
wishes of landsmen to worship together. At each Passover, every
member of the family was dressed in new clothes, no matter how
crippling the expense or the debt incurred. One of the earliest
Leylands synagogues was over a stable and there little crocodiles
of stiffly correct families would make their way each sabbath, to
worship together with those elders who could remember the old,
ruinous past. The melting-pot was deep and turbulent, much more
emotionally spiced than the everday Leylands itself suggested.

The area was depressing and uninspiring, to put it mildly.
There is a half-ashamed memory among many Leeds families
today of walking down to the Leylands to stare in astonishment at
something new and strange. Leeds was not a remarkably law-
8

University extensions

abiding society at the time, and the Leylands was no Snob Hill. In a few mean streets just over the hill from the Headrow something very important to Leeds was beginning. If you looked only at the streets and the neighbourhood, things looked black. The story of the Jews in Leeds is the story of their successful assimilation.

In the early 1900s, a new road forced through the packed houses of the Leylands broke up its homogeneity as a Jewish quarter. Among the streets to be levelled there was Hope Street, probably the most poignant street name in Leeds Jewish memory. The hub of the Leylands was Byron Street, which still exists as a roadway. Little of the character it had then could be guessed at now. There was there a leather store and grindery which supplied and serviced the slipper-makers and cobblers. In houses round about tailors renewed a cottage industry of garment manufacture, each house specializing in a particular part of the whole, so that the trousers joined the jacket of a suit only at the very end of the process. In other house-shops, bakers would clear away their workday trade for the special baking of matzos for Passover.

Dispersal from the Leylands was forced on Jews by the new road and the demolition of the Hope Street housing. They moved a little further north up the Meanwood Valley, gradually leapfrogging away from the old, original quarter. In Lovell Road, the Jewish community found what it was looking for above all else. It found an institution and a person to match its own driving energy.

Lovell Road Council School was, without exaggeration, the university of the original Leeds Jewry. Its headmaster, Thomas Bentley, was a Christian who found his school first surrounded, and then invested, by the Jewish population moving out of the Leylands. Bentley was a man in his prime, with heavy Edwardian moustaches and impeccable manners and dress. By any standards he was a remarkable man. By the standards of his day, he was already a superlative head-teacher.

Children were put to school in the Leylands often before they were three. If the household was also a workshop, as it so often was, there was nowhere else to go. Children shared boots, the older child carrying the younger, barefoot sister or brother through the streets. Families were large in size with often as many as ten children under one roof. The father and mother worked by

day and night. In this situation, the school was at the very least
a place to store the children.

Bentley did more, much more. He seems to have been a
completely no-nonsense man in a crisis period when weakness,
indifference, or dislike would have proved disastrous. Bentley
forced on his school qualities which were already a part of his
pupils' characters. Chief among these was pride. He was himself
a proud, strict but gentle man, and he made quite sure that his
ideas of a community were enforced. Every child in his school
paid him a penny a week. With this money he introduced violin
lessons and bought the school a lantern slide projector. He had a
bowl of goldfish put into the hall and hung the walls with colour
reproductions of the most stirring episodes of British history. He
wrote plays and had them acted. He was famous for paying as
much attention to a child's boots as to his brains. He was com-
passionate and he was ambitious. His children loved him.

Lovell Road School broke records year after year for scholarship successes. Bentley's standing in the community was
demonstrated on his retirement by the presents and gifts showered
on him. He was by no means a famous figure of Leeds education
but to this day it is reckoned by anyone who remembers the
Leylands at first-hand that Lovell Road has indirectly supplied
the city with many of its best solicitors, doctors and accountants.
Bentley's ambition was for his pupils rather than himself. His
immigrants were perhaps special cases, but in their own estima-
tion, he was a remarkable teacher of immigrants. He took the
children of Landsmen and he opened the door for them into the
whole of Leeds. For some, he showed them the whole world.

Jews were soon generally admired by official opinion for their
industry and adapability to the new life. Almost a third of the
total immigration to Britain settled in Leeds, some by choice,
some who always intended to go on to America. The diversity
of job opportunity in Leeds and their own grit lifted Leeds
Jewry from the Leylands to a full place in the life of the city.
Moving first to the North Street area, and then into the villas of
Chapeltown and later into the new suburbs of Moortown,
Roundhay, and Alwoodley, Leeds Jewry has advanced to a
position of great confidence and capacity. The population has
shrunk from its highest point at 1907, but the influence it exerts

in Leeds is more powerful for being more widely dispersed.
The full history of the Jews in Leeds has yet to be written. It will
need to come, not from an economist or sociologist but from the
man who remembers the teeming, restless humanity of the Leylands, and can make that live. It is a remarkable story, too long
suppressed, perhaps for reasons of reticence that go hand in hand
with pride in Jewish life.

The Jews moved to Chapeltown as their prosperity rose. The
district is a triangle of housing on the other side of the valley to
North Lane, where their life and livelihood was first located. The
road divides itself between the road up the Meanwood Valley and
the high roads to Harrogate and Roundhay. A hundred years ago
it was chiefly known for its cavalry barracks. Rookie dragoons
could see the new gasworks from one end of the ridge and the
new poorhouse from the other. All the rest was fields and farms.

Although the ward boundaries of present-day Chapeltown are
more extensive than the Harrogate Road–Roundhay Road–
Harehills Lane triangle, it is this area which most people think of
as 'Chapeltown'. It forms a natural enclave. The Jews made
Chapeltown dense with houses in their slow progress northwards
out of the city. As they left it was occupied in turn by other
immigrants and minority groups. Within half a mile here are
synagogues, a Sikh temple, a Polish ex-Servicemen's club and a
Lithuanian Association. But in present-day Chapeltown, the
majority of faces are black. It is a quarter principally but not
entirely occupied by West Indian immigrants.

So much nonsense has been written about coloured immigrants
to Britain that it would need a book to explain their settlement in
Leeds. A good part of that book would be a vigorous defence.
In just such a book in a Leeds suburban library, someone has
annotated the text with occasional pencil comments. The hand-
writing is a woman's neat and clerkly. Against a passage on
Jewish religious life is written, "Jews stick together." Against a
passage on job opportunities for West Indians is written, "This is
OUR country." The two comments nicely sum up a particular
kind of racial intolerance. In the face of the Jewish presence there
is a certain caution and oblique dislike. Blacks are easier to attack,
perhaps because they have not the guard and stance that Jews have
learned from centuries of bitter experience.

A Leeds man is captured by African cannibals [*sic*]. As he goes
into the pot, one says, "Where do you come from then?" When
he is told, the cannibal says, "Oh yes? Do you know if our kid has
got his council house in Bradford yet?" This is only a good-
natured joke if one can presume the good nature of its victim.
That this is the case with West Indians is entirely to their credit,
not at all to ours. The emotional generosity of West Indian
immigrants may be their worst enemy. In Leeds, which is a
phlegmatic city even by the high standards of phlegm set in the
county as a whole, West Indians, Sikhs and the small population
of Pakistanis get by without great conflict. There has been no
serious expression of racial intolerance in Leeds and with luck
there will be none.

The repatriation of the coloured community in Leeds (to which
the present government is committed in principle) may prove a
good deal more difficult to implement than its author, Enoch
Powell, supposes. There is no question but that all coloured
minorities are disadvantaged in Leeds, as they are anywhere else.
Leeds was no more geared to the permanent settlement of a
coloured population than any other city in Britain. It is difficult to
see how it could have been. Yet it has managed to elude the
scaremongering politician whose aim is to make a difficult
situation impossible. The panic-in-the-streets future for Britain
is very hard to realise imaginatively in Leeds. Left to itself, the
city will accommodate the change in itself that is necessary to
acknowledge the civic rights of coloured Yorkshiremen. It is
true that the most testing times have yet to come. It is true that an
economic recession could change everything overnight. But
Leeds has as good a chance as anywhere else in Britain—and
better than most—to make the change. The test is whether it *is*
left to itself.

Chapeltown is no great trailer for the great rivers of blood
spectacular said to be coming shortly. It looks like any other part
of Leeds, except that the great majority of its tenants are coloured.
It is otherwise no more colourful or exotic than any other
working-class district. You would need to be exceptionally
sentimental to romanticize Chapeltown as a little chunk of
Caribbean sunshine set down in the Industrial North. In fact you
would need an inverted racial discrimination more common in

London. You will see Jamaicans standing about gossiping far longer than any Northerner would consider practical. Tiny children totter past with polythene sacks of laundry which seem to contain the entire household effects and the occasional exquisitely beautiful girl is driven past by a cool, cool man. But Chapeltown as a piece of Leeds exotica is about as realistic as describing Alwoodley as a seething Jewish conspiracy. It is a complete non-starter.

The coloured community does not even live in Chapeltown principally. It is more widely dispersed through the Meanwood Valley and over the ridge into Burley, rich Headingley's poor neighbour. This dispersal is static at the moment, but the spread of coloured communities, even among working-class districts, makes the operation of an open colour bar difficult. Pubs that have tried to operate one have had their managers removed with lightning speed. It is simply the case in Leeds that colour is not an issue. When xenophobic politicians give dire warnings for the future they have a special significance for this city. The race is not to prevent full integration from taking place but to accomplish it before the rivers of blood are talked into existence. Fortunately for everyone in Leeds, the people there are a bit suspicious of folk who just *talk* about it, whether it is race, Rugby League or rhubarb-forcing.

X

THE ARTS

THE cultural wilderness that is supposed to exist beyond the reach of London's red buses is believed by Londoners to be progressively bleaker the further north the hapless traveller blunders. It is not clear and never has been exactly what the provinces lack. Confusion may be based on a provincial mis-apprehension about London itself as the centre of a high culture of theatre, films, opera, books, music, and galleries and museums.

Leeds suffers from the wound of being thought a vulgar sort of place to live, and in common with other provincial cities has to some extent inflicted the injury on itself. For of course London is no more cultured than anywhere else, except in the sense of being the centre for places where the old idea of culture as "the world of ideas embodied in the arts" has its sway. In any serious and meaningful use of the word, Leeds probably has rather more of liveliness in its culture than many parts of London. But of course it is part of the wound for cities like Leeds to ignore this more positive definition of its cultural stock and pine instead for the great lack of this, that or the other that is reportedly ten a penny in the great metropolis.

It has suffered these pangs of anxiety for generations. In the nineteenth century, it was uncultured in the sense of being un-refined. Robert Lowe, who had charge of education in the period 100 years ago when Leeds could be said to have turned a corner, asked the House of Commons, "You have had the opportunity of knowing some of the constituencies of this country, and I ask, if you want ignorance, if you want drunkenness and facility for being intimidated; or if on the other hand you want impulsive, unreflecting and violent people, where do you look for them in the constituencies? Do you go to the top or to the bottom?" He might have added that there were constituencies and constituencies. It is a nice snobbishness on the part of many people today to prefer a fistfight outside a Cornish pub to a fistfight outside a pub in the Dewsbury Road. One's more elegant than another, somehow, if you have to fight at all.

Leeds was a dangerous place to live for outsiders. They used to wait on Leeds bridge at the foot of Briggate for the actors to come by. It was great fun to toss these over into the Aire. In the nineteenth century the schools inspectors could find nothing much to write home about in the education of their charges. By much dinning into, the children learned their tables and could recite the simple facts of history on which our heritage is founded, but were woefully lacking in any sort of refinement. Refinement is a hard commodity to come by in a city built almost entirely as a business speculation. Leeds had and has no patrons, no men of great substance who want not only a house but a beautiful house. The Assembly Rooms in York are exquisite, perfect, considered by some architects to be among the best of interiors in Europe. But York has more than its fair share of great patronage. Leeds has less than its share. Refinement cannot be borrowed, It is learned.

If you cannot be refined, you had better guard against the worser fate still of being ridiculed. T. S. Eliot, casting about for a simile of awkwardness, wrote in *The Waste Land* of something being awkward as "the silk hat on the head of a Bradford millionaire". To Leeds as well as to Bradford, that casual joke goes much deeper than the surface. It goes home to a deep fear of being held to ridicule. In this sense, Leeds shares the same guilt as any other large city in Britain: a guilt at being provincial at all. The use of the adjective provincial as a term of abuse dates from the heyday of Leeds's growth.

There is an interesting possibility that part of the ignorance shown about Leeds may stem from its own shame. It has little to be ashamed of and a great deal to recommend it as a place to live. But when Matthew Arnold raised the spectre of Philistinism, he could hardly have guessed how much hurt he would do the new cities emerging, which he above all knew of better than many of his contemporaries. Arnold was an inspector of schools from 1851 to 1886. The sort of schools he was used to visiting were nothing like Rugby, where he had been with his illustrious father as headmaster. Yet Arnold's view of education was that it was a purgation of the gross, and his view of culture that it was essentially refinement. The awful solemnness of his ideas tended to stop people in their tracks before they could go out and exercise the beautiful thoughts he gave them. Arnold unwittingly made the word culture a dirty word for a majority of Englishmen and sowed a seed of doubt in many a city council's breast. Few could match his high standards.

Neither was there much solace in consulting that other high master of refinement, John Ruskin. In 1859 Ruskin was invited to speak at the School of Design in Bradford. How many invitations went out to neighbouring Leeds to hear this amazing piece of hysteria.

I must necessarily ask you, how much of [England] do you seriously intend within the next fifty years to be coal-pit, brick-field, or quarry? For the sake of distinctness of conclusion I will suppose your success absolute: that from shore to shore the whole of the island is to be set as thick with chimnies as the masts stand in the docks of Liverpool; that there shall be no meadows in it; no trees, no gardens, only a little corn grown upon the housetops, reaped and threshed by steam; that you do not intend to leave even room for roads, but travel either over the roofs of your mills on viaducts, or under their floors in tunnels; that the smoke having rendered the light of the sun unserviceable, you work always by the light of your own gas; that no acre of English land shall be without its shaft and its engine; and therefore no spot of English ground left, on which it shall be possible to stand, without a definite and calculable risk of being blown off it, at any moment, into small pieces.

Under these conditions, Ruskin advised, the country would no need culture any more than it needed Schools of Design. His attack contains some interesting points, not least the apparent inability to see that those who are for him the perpetrators of such ugliness are also its first and principal victims.

Today, the old confusions of purpose and attitude described in the bombshell word 'culture' seem likely to be blown away in harmless smoke. The thing to say about the Northern environment is that it is—in places—grossly inadequate. Ruskin managed to say this with more than a hint that it was also uncultured. He forgot his own precepts elsewhere. The dullness and blight he saw around him on his Northern tour was as much the fault of gentlemanly indolence in high places of government as it was the result of common rapacity on the mill floor. The idea that culture was to do with vague higher beauties of the mind has led to the ridiculous belief that many people will die with, that Ruskin's vision was fulfilled and the North is now one long Coronation Street from end to end and coast to coast. Because it was not worth coming to see for oneself, the idea grew up that it was all physical ugliness. This myth is now as outdated as the Northern councillor's counter-assertion that "if yon culture has to do wi' pictures, then get us a few for t'Town Hall, Mr. Town Clerk, lad".

Because these ideas have been a long time dying, imitative art and architecture is still plentiful in Leeds. In the earlier period, when Leeds was eager for recognition as being at any rate something like London (and so ancient Athens and Rome) there is something delightful about the aping that went on. This is an account of a club a near-gentleman could hope to join, one where his want of landed inheritance could perhaps be overlooked.

The Society of Yorkshire Archers held their October meeting on Monday last, at Chapel Town, near the place [Leeds]. The shooting was good, in spite of a very high wind. At three o'clock, after a severe struggle, Lord Fitzwilliam's silver bugle was determined to be won by Thomas Wybergh, Esq., who was captain of the target and lieutenant of numbers. Alexander Pitcairn, Esq., was captain of numbers and lieutenant of the targets. The society dined at the bowling green house, and spent the remainder of the day, as usual in mirth and conviviality.

To this picture of an activity one must add in houses in the gentlemanly style, decorations and furnishings according to the tastes of the quality, and accomplishments and manners that bespoke refinement. If the Yorkshire Society of Archers was no match for the Court of St. James, no matter; the eighteenth century was delightfully unabashed by its own snobbishness. It experienced no shame. Time and again in the *Leeds Intelligencer* for the period one comes across references which refer unblushingly to Leeds things as "among the finest there ever was in the nation", "generally reckoned to be of the most delicate taste", and so on. If it was aping, it was helpful and it was done unself-

consciously. It made something where nothing was. The Leeds
Gentlemen Volunteer Corps received their colours in 1792:

> On Friday last the Leeds Gentlemen Volunteer Corps had a grand
> field day for the purpose of receiving their colours. At nine o'clock
> in the morning the corps paraded in the White Cloth Hall yard, and
> marched from thence to Chapel Town Moor, where an immense
> concourse of people were assembled to be present at the ceremony,
> which was solemn, impressive, and pleasing. The colours were con-
> veyed to the field in cases, under an escort of serjeants; and being
> unfurled, were then presented by Mrs Mayoress, and Mrs Lloyd;
> after which Samuel Buck, Esq., the Recorder, in a short but expres-
> sive speech, exhorted the corps to guard these military ensigns, thus
> prepared and given by the ladies. The different companies then
> formed a circle and the colours being placed in the centre upon the
> drums, the Rev. Pter Haddon, our Vicar and their Chaplain, pro-
> ceeded to the consecration. . . . After the delivery of this excellent
> prayer, the corps went through their manouevres with great eclat,
> and fired three vollies that would have done honour to a veteran
> regiment. The ladies were accommodated with a marqué and were
> treated by Captain Lloyd with tea, coffee, cake, etc. The corps
> returned to town about three o'clock and at four sat down in the
> Concert Room to an excellent dinner given by Alex Turner, Esq.,
> the Mayor. . . . Many excellent songs were given by Mr Meredith,
> who in God Save the King and Rule Brittania displayed his wonder-
> ful powers of voice with the most astonishing effect, and who added
> much to the pleasure of the afternoon.

That kind of refinement was followed by exquisite contortions
of taste as Leeds lost its grip on what it was it was supposed to
imitate. Today, the situation is far happier. No one can be
completely satisfied with Leeds as a centre for the arts, but few
would waste time on believing that what was missing was
irremediable or had to do with birthplace or origins. The old idea
of culture gets short shrift in Leeds today. Our view of culture
has changed with a changing education and is a little more dynamic than what it was. There was a time in which this chapter
might have pointed desperately to a few worthy museum relics
and gallery collections as something of virtue in a dirty environment.

The Leeds Playhouse is the newest theatre in the North of
England and the revival of repertory theatre in the city after many

years' absence. It opened in a blaze of notoriety, with a production of a play by Alan Plater, the Hull writer. *Simon Says* was a calculated attack on middle-class values and used as a main plank in its platform farcical treatment of that religious solemnity in Yorkshire, cricket. At its first night a local M.P. walked out, followed by some indignant citizens. The Lord Mayor was only constrained to stay in his seat by a sense of civic duty. *Simon Says* was not a 'nice' play and it hurt quite as much as was intended. Perhaps more so, for the theatre gained an unwanted reputation for being 'difficult' and 'flippant', words which weigh heavy in Yorkshire. It must be all the more galling to the intrepid management of the Playhouse to find itself attacked from the opposite direction. Shortly after *Simon Says* opened, the gala opening was performed by Prince Charles (he saw *Oh Glorious Jubilee*, a tame, jolly production he might have graced himself, using his experience of undergraduate revue). A week or so after this royal visit, the Playhouse wall was decorated with the anonymous slogan "smash bourgeois art" to which was added, in the same neat letters "long live working-class culture"! This impromptu criticism nicely sums up the problem of culture in contemporary Leeds, taken in conjunction with the huffing and puffing of the civic dignitaries earlier.

The Playhouse is more of a people's theatre than either set of critics tend to realize. The civic authorities have by no means made the path smooth for professional repertory in Leeds, and the working classes (whoever they are) have not contributed in any great bulk to the appeal which financed the theatre. In fact, the best friend of the trustees has been the university, who provided the shell-building on a site within the campus, for a lease of ten years. Almost the whole of the rest of the energy which went into the creation of the Playhouse has come from the public, under the restless, talented direction of a team of local people who wished to add theatre to the community assets. Theatres are not cheap to build and staff; and the provincial theatre which was thought to be on the boom in the 'sixties is going to face some problems in the 'seventies.

It is all the more interesting therefore that the Playhouse has come into being in this specific, hard-edged, limited fashion, as a sort of community speculation. Theatres are especially sensitive to criticism and their commercial viability is always in conflict with their artistic pretensions. To suppose otherwise, in either direction, is stupid. The direction of plays is not so important as the will which creates and maintains the building. To commit oneself to the building of a new professional theatre in Leeds is a hardy and courageous act. The physical presence of the Playhouse in Leeds says much for the thousands who subscribed to it. The repertory of plays and their direction is something else, another argument.

The people who walked out from *Simon Says* had perhaps different expectations of community theatre. Their view of the theatre was perhaps passive. The plain fact is that any form of arts activity in the provinces needs active support—really active involvement. This is not because the provinces are 'philistine' but simply because the potential audiences for one or other art are so much smaller than in London. Without the tourists who flock to London, many theatres there would close. The Playhouse was built on the premise that people who had never experienced a regular company playing in a repertory of lively plays could hardly comment on whether they would like one in Leeds. Its task is to build support. Because the potential audience is smaller, the support has to be more intense.

Critics of the Playhouse have pointed out that there already existed a theatre in Leeds, the Grand. The council itself was inclined to agree. Although it hedged its bet with a comparatively small grant to the Playhouse, there were many councillors who saw no essential difference between it and the existing Grand. A grant went to it, too.

The Grand is a large auditorium which survived the plight of its other competitors, all but one of which have disappeared. The Grand is a try-out theatre for West End plays and the venue of large touring productions. It is the sole remaining place for the big spectacular and the classical repertory of the national companies. It has, of course, a quite different function to the Playhouse and meets a quite different need. It is no unkindness to say of the Grand that it is for the people who can take theatre or leave it alone, who have no allegiance to the technique of acting and production but like a good tale, or a grand spectacle. They may incidentally be moved by an experience they could get in no other way, but that is not their chief purpose in going. Sell-out houses for an appalling tour of *Hair* and an empty theatre for the exquisite Sierra Leone Dance Company are an indication of what a purely commercial theatre must hassle with.

The most famous theatre in Leeds is the Famous City Varieties, rescued from an obscure but honourable grave by the phenominal success of the television show broadcast from the stage. The City Varieties is the most beautiful theatre in Leeds, and with far and away the most atmosphere. All the music-hall greats played the Varieties, including such people noted in the firm's book as "G. Robey, Scots Comic". Barney Colehan's nostalgic productions for the BBC of *Old-Time Music Hall* released an unspoken affection for the 'Good Old Days' which surprised everybody except the Joseph brothers whose family theatre this has been. The Varieties has been assured by the success of its television appearances a future that is otherwise against the odds. It is likely that the theatre itself, quite apart from the shows, will become a place of homage for those who like their nostalgia mixed with the smell of greasepaint. Few of these small Edwardian music-halls survive and Leeds is lucky to have one intact at its very centre.

We must not leave the professional drama without mentioning the value to the whole region of having in Leeds the Northern Drama Department of BBC radio. Under the direction of Alfred Bradley this has given encouragement to writers and actors all over Yorkshire and done as much as anyone to lift the region to a new confidence in its own talent. Radio drama is not a difficult or expensive form of radio and there is no reason why it should not flourish anywhere in Britain. That it has done so in Leeds under Alfred Bradley is entirely due to his imagination, drive and enthusiasm. Inside the profession, as many people remember Leeds for its radio drama as for anything else. The number of writers discovered and helped along by the BBC in Leeds is a tribute to skilful and patient patronage of the highest order.

There is a strong tradition of amateur drama. Broderick's Civic Institute was made eventually into a Civic Theatre. Many of the leading lights of the amateur stage were among the staunchest supporters for professional repertory. Alec Baron, whose productions for the Proscenium Players were the high point of many a winter, became the Leeds Playhouse's first general manager. It was in the Civic that the theatre appeal was launched, with some of the most famous names in theatre mixing with dedicated amateurs.

The university has its own little theatre which services performances from all over the campus and is the home of the drama department of the School of English. Student theatre in Leeds has had fame far outside the walls of the university and a production won the Student Drama Festival in Zagreb in 1967. The School of English has followed the BBC in encouraging the work of young and new writers for its theatre. If one remembers that there are extremely well-established theatres in York, Harrogate and above all Sheffield; and lively Little Theatres in the commuter towns of Otley and Ilkley, the condition of theatre in and around Leeds is by no means as low as its critics suppose.

The 'theatre renaissance' in Britain is likely to tread a much more difficult path than enthusiasts inside and outside theatres ever supposed. The first real shock to the new management of the Playhouse was a 100 per cent Equity pay increase, which the manager was quick to admit was "thoroughly well-merited". The problems are not only financial, however; they are a complete mix of financial and artistic issues. What can be claimed for theatre in Leeds is that it has at any rate brought out into open discussion some of the more absurd arguments—on both sides—about cultural poverty and philistinism. In Leeds, both parties, the philistine and the aesthete, are having to shift from their old typecast positions of bullnecked wrath and pale mauve indignation.

We have been so consumed with the debate about 'minority' and 'mass culture', cross hatched with all the rest about 'London' and 'provincial' tastes, it has escaped the attention of some of the cultural gestapo that ordinary people are quite capable of enjoying and participating in great works of art, without much caring what their provenance is. This is particularly so of music. Yorkshire is a great county for choral music. It is also famous for its love of brass among the instruments of the orchestra; it has produced no great concert orchestras, but it has great choirs and a tradition of great popular music-making. Amateurs of music abound in the county, with a knowledge and expertise that has given nothing but good to professional music. (Frye might have reflected on the success of a policy his own government adopted, to encourage instrument-tuition among the general population.) In all events, Leeds has a very creditable standing as a centre for serious music. In this context, serious means just what it says.

It is true that this standing has been enhanced by the personal interest shown in music by the Earl of Harewood, patron of the Leeds Triennal Music Festival. As president of Leeds United, A.F.C., in addition, he will be the first to acknowledge the foundation of solid study and practice his own efforts have built upon. Music in Leeds as in any other west Yorkshire town is a common pleasure. The pomp and glitter of the great occasion is only the topping on a long tradition.

The Triennial and the International Pianoforte competition are the great occasions. For the latter, Leeds has to thank one of the most gifted teachers of piano in the county, Miss Fanny Waterman, O.B.E. Fanny Waterman has the knack of discovering star pianists—Michael Rolls was a pupil of hers—without the apparatus of a musical academy. The international competition has attracted more attention to Leeds from the musical world than any other event. It joins the Triennial as an established and warmly awaited date in the musical calendar.

So certain of the public it seeks is the festival that it has no particular need to encourage the fringe and by so doing widen its appeal. Like the York Festival, it is primarily a festival of music. Unlike the York Festival, it has a peculiarly local and immediate atmosphere that stems from strong roots in amateur musical activity. There is not a 'class' audience for music in Leeds and the city is mercifully free of the sort of black-tie social occasions which are also musical entertainments. We can see something of the vitality of the tradition from the number of local music teachers who are also composers. The Music Centre, the university department of music, the lunch-hour recitals in the art gallery and a host of choirs are also witness. There has been a Leeds Philharmonic for more than a century; the very first music festival was brought into being for the Queen's visit in 1858. (The programme concluded with, of course and as a point of local honour, the *Messiah*, practically a Yorkshire anthem.)

As for sculpture, it too is in a state of health, The City Square is not especially the place to look for the best examples. Hamilton Thompson, a professor of mediaeval archaeology in the university forty years ago, was moved from his usual constraint and academic

Seacroft Centre steelwork
Roundhay Park ironwork

dignity to write of City Square: "If there is some discrepancy between the Black Prince on his charger and the dishevelled ladies who hold lamps upon the circumference of the circle, and still less community of sentiment between these nymphs and the four worthies who decorously turn their backs on them to contemplate and address their proclamations to the austere façade of the General Post Office, the combination of statutory is at any rate original."

The new sculpture is livelier for being more ingenious. Austin Dalwood's large aluminium relief is unfortunately tucked away from the general view on the wall of Bodington, a university hall of residence. In Sweet Street, on the outside wall of a wholesale warehouse, is an extremely good-looking architectural mural, commissioned from Harry Thubron by Bernard Gillinson. There is another Dalwood in the congress of the Merrion Centre and at Seacroft a whole range of architectural shapes and structures, commissioned by the authority from its own architects.

Probably the greatest artist of any kind the area will even produce is Henry Moore, born at Castleford in 1898. Moore studied at Leeds College of Art, and tells an interesting story of the lay figures used in preference to the living model at that time. His eye told him that something was wrong with the proportions of these figures, although he could not place exactly where his anxiety was most merited. At the end of the year these plaster figures were cleaned of coat upon coat of whitewash, and Moore realized that he had been staring at forms thickened out by generations of well-intended painting.

Although many other influences came to bear on his work, Moore's sculpture has an irreducible humanity and gravity which is easily recognizable by anyone who knows his northern landscape. The City Art Gallery has some examples of his work, including a superb reclining figure and some fascinating maquettes for larger works.

The department of fine art in the university was set up with the help of Eric Gregory, a printer. Gregory's interest in fine art was not simply historical. He endowed fellowships in painting, sculpture and poetry at the same time, which ensured a close contract between the university and practising artists. In 1943, when the Gregory Fellowships were created, they were a brilliant

9

The last of the ancient Meanwood Beck

initiative and act of faith. Gregory's inspiration has been justified a dozen times over. In fact, one of the most interesting Gregory fellows of recent years has been yet another sculptor, Neville Boden. Of the poetry fellows, Jon Silkin and Bill Turner have been particularly successful in extending the popularity of poetry by teaching and readings.

When Henry Moore was at the school of art, he was the first sculpture student ever admitted. In fact they created the department for him. In the period after the Second World War, Leeds became one of the leading art schools in the county. It even had a considerable international reputation. Leeds became a power-house college, thanks to the brilliant development of further education by the Education Department. This, linked with the sort of teaching the department was able to attract, made the college of art in particular into a really vital institution. It has produced a stream of gifted young teachers and artists.

In case this sounds like the whitewash on a plaster saint, it is worth reflecting on the sources of a city's artistic standing. Great artists alone do not make a milieu. Moore has been one of the most forthcoming writers we have had in the plastic arts, yet he has lived comparatively quietly and in isolation from a specific community. A great musician like Menuhin can make a pleasure city like Bath of great importance in the musical world at large; but could either Moore or Menuhin make an industrial city conscious and active in the arts, at every level, simply by living among the people?

Leeds College of Art, the Music Centre, and all the educational institutions of the city, do something all the more important for being aimed lower than the attainment of a few gifted individuals. Despite the comparative actual poverty of the region, Yorkshire is an education-hungry county. Some of this is the natural and necessary hunger of people without bread in their mouths. Some of it is a need that has been awakened by the driving energies of educationists. The college of art is difficult to single out in this argument, which is not so much about excellence (although this happened) but about civic responsibility. That said, it would not be Yorkshire if a hundred teachers did not turn round and claim that they did it in spite of the Education Office.

The rise of Temple Newsam under civic care is however

another example of the same thing. Temple Newsam was originally founded as a preceptory of Knights Templar by Henry de Lacy in the middle of the twelve century. It then passed to the D'Arcy family until the time of the Pilgrimage of Grace in the reign of Henry VIII. The object of the Pilgrimage of the Yorkshire Catholic gentry to London was to restore the sovereign to his religious obligations. Lord D'Arcy was one of those captured and peremptorily executed on Tower Hill. Henry gave the house to the Earl of Lennox. Their son Henry, Lord Darnley, was born here. Darnley married Mary Queen of Scots and was the unlucky father of James I. His wife's countrymen blew him to pieces in an Edinburgh house. (They later beheaded her.)

The present house was built on the site of the old by Sir Arthur Ingram in 1629, and stayed in one family for the next 300 years. Temple Newsam is of Leeds but not Leeds. It lies at the extreme south-eastern boundary of the present city overlooking the Aire and was considered in its time to be the finest brick building in the county. The coal measures run under the estate and Temple Newsam must have been one of the few great houses of England with a colliery in its grounds.

Under municipal direction Temple Newsam is now one of the best collections of decorative art in the country. It is a quality collection, something very much more than a museum and a credit to the city. It says a great deal for Leeds that in matters like this the corporation can make provisions which would not disgrace a national government. It is a curiosity of the city that Temple Newsam and Kirkstall Abbey—which also has a museum area—are among the few clear remains of the city which pre-date the Industrial Revolution. It is pleasant to record that both are exceptionally good.

The creation of the Yorkshire Arts Association has already done a great deal to encourage artistic activity by grant-in-aid. The association has been particularly helpful in popularizing and bringing within 'establishment' art the new arts now developing. In Leeds, it is not the town hall that has turned out to be the most philistine influence, but if anything the very people who are most anxious to perpetuate the cloth-cap-and-whippet image of public service—the cultural élite of the students, particularly the university. It is said that the university of Leeds Students' Union has more than £250,000 at its disposal at any one time. What it does with the money is extremely poorly advertised, seldom exciting, and very often culturally empty.

Leeds is a community with an extremely sensitive feeling for place. Its art, like its football, has to be local and immediate. The Gregory Fellowships are one of the few cultural links the young of the city have with their university. It is depressing otherwise to note how little the student activity of the university flows over into the working life of the place which gave it so much. There is of course no special obligation on an undergraduate body to its host town. On the other hand, the undergraduates of Leeds could probably do very much more than has been done in the past. The university should be one of those material benefits to the community it resides among that confirms civic pride and attracts new blood. Among politically conscious students the view has been expressed (as slogans on convenient walls) that what is needed is student–worker alliance. The young industrial worker in Leeds has no special reason to look to his contemporaries within the university for help. One of the richest foundations of money for what he is interested in has hardly extended its influence beyond the university walls. The old philistinism dies hard. A smattering of sociological jargon does not altogether disguise it. If the student who sprayed the Playhouse with his "Smash bourgeois art" could point to its alternative, ideologically correct or otherwise, anywhere in the dealings of his own kind with young Leeds, one could take his criticism a little more in earnest.

XI

UNITED! UNITED!

IT IS a fine sunny day in October. South Leeds is agitated like a gigantic ants' nest. Cars ride bumper to bumper from all directions and the streets off Elland Road are a vast park of cars with registrations from all over Yorkshire and the North of England. On foot, a steady stream of men and boys tramp on resolutely and steadily. The younger smaller boys carry homemade boxes and stools. Today Leeds United play Manchester United at home.

Nearer the ground, police and bus officials are dealing competently but a bit white-faced with the onrush of 50,000 fans. The ground capacity is 53,000, a figure calculated afresh each season for the club by the police. About £20,000 will change hands in the next thirty minutes and the gate will be one of the best of the season. Manchester United, low in the table, playing without Denis Law, are still one of the most charismatic sides in the League. They are lending some of their glamour to Leeds for the afternoon. It is to be like the cheeky, artful kid taking on the tough, silent kid in the school playground.

There are police everywhere, more police than most of the crowd will ever see in the streets in their lifetime. To a stranger so many police are a shock. The fans ignore them altogether. On their side, the young constables guarding the turnstiles do their best to look bored and indifferent. It is a difficult face to keep up, because the air crackles with electric tension. On the Kop the fans roar out sentimental songs with appalling changes in the lyrics, and clap in unison like thunder. For the latecomers the roar that greets the arrival of the teams on the pitch spurs them to a run. The turnstiles clatter frantically.

Despite improvements, Leeds's ground is not particularly big, nor is it sumptuously appointed. The latecomers to the Kop run to the top of the steps which lead on to the terraces. The whole stand is a dense mass of people. The favours are pretty equally divided between red and white; there is an ominous dividing gap down the terraces to keep actual riot from breaking out. Near at hand the atmosphere is good-natured enough but there is an air of truculence over the whole Kop that is terrifying. From time to time a surge carries the crowd down the terraces ten yards or more. While the nervous, the weak and the short cry out in alarm or vexation, a youth fights with his elbows for room to eat his pie and drink his carton of scalding hot Bovril. It is something like mixing a whisky and soda in the Hawaiian surf or lighting a cigarette in the middle of an avalanche. Only a real fan would try it.

'Nesh' is a Yorkshire word meaning soft. Before a ball has been kicked in the game, about 200 spectators who could be called nesh are back at the foot of the stairs under the Kop. The lucky ones have seen the pitch and the extra lucky ones seen the laconic George Best warming up. Most have paid all and seen nowt. A man has brought out his young wife, who must be at least six months pregnant. She leans against the wall, greyer than the concrete. Parents pacify their small sons who have been buffeted silly but are all for plunging back up the stairs. One lad holds his folding stool forlornly at the trail-arms position. Nobody up on the terraces can see the ground they are standing on, let alone make room for a flimsy stool.

There is a tea bar down here in the cavernous underside of the Kop, but who could get out to use it? The idle tea girls watch as their only customer, a boy of about eighteen, sinks slowly to his knees and keels over, as if shot by a gamewarden with a sleep-dart. The young policemen who were outside checking the turnstiles are now inside checking the cashiers. One of them strolls over to the boy on the ground. Whatever he says is lost in a fantastic barrage of noise, more of a howl than a cheer, a deep-throated animal howl, shatteringly resonant. Shortly after the start of the match, someone in the crowds has blown a whistle. Manchester United stop playing, Leeds do not. Jackie Charlton nods the ball into the net with that strange nonchalance the big man has, and the referee allows the goal.

Shortly after, the casualties of sport begin to stumble back downstairs. A boy is led down with a gash in his head through which the white bone shows. A dozen separate streams of blood crack open his shocked face. He has a red and white scarf round his neck. Must feel a very long way from Manchester at this moment. A police constable takes him away gently and compassionately.

Refugees keep coming down. A young girl skinhead appears. Her hair is crewcut on top but left long at the sides, an effect startling enough to look like a scalping. Jeans, braces, bovver boots. All of fourteen years old. Trying not to cry. But her appearance is something extra bizarre. Most of the nesh milling about under the stand are ordinary folk trapped in a little bit of English mania. They are a remarkably phlegmatic group, reckoning the price of admission at 7s. 6d. a head. None of the people waiting to be let out of the locked gates have seen a single second of the match. A minute or so before half time, police unlock the gates. "Who's going to give us us money back?" a collier shouts.

"Not me, mate," the inspector in charge says. "You'll have to see the club about that."

But few do. There is a heated argument at the entrance to a tunnel leading back into the ground at the level of the paddocks. A few outraged fans heckle the police, who parry with extreme good humour. Just above head level, from small windows protected by heavy mesh, there is a frantic hollow barking. "What's score, what's score?" from hoarse voices. The windows look out from the police cells. Even under arrest, the team comes first.

The sun has crept lower unnoticed. It is now misty and autumnal round the approaches to the ground. More prudent men will have worked their allotments on a day like this, or taken the wife shopping for a bit of carpet or new wellies for the kids. But there are still a few late arrivals, even though the second half has started. A few lads choose a particularly hair-raising way to climb into the stand for nowt, pursued by an equally reckless policeman. And of course, there are a few maniacs who have walked a mile or so just to see the teams come out after it's all over and the crowd has gone home. Just to see the heroes, or shout a word or two, or even touch them on the back.

On the bus going home, the only question asked of the nesh is, inevitably: "What's score?"

A couple of Saturday mornings later, St. Edmund's Roundhay Cub Scouts are taking on the local rivals. What seems like half a hundred little boys run after the ball with relentless energy. With this level soccer, each side is good for five goals apiece. Double figures are taken for granted when the duffers play the ace side. It's all in the game. The day is saturated with fine rain that has had only a very short way to fall—the cloud is apparently resting on the top of the trees across the Soldiers' Field.

A large white Mercedes pulls up and for twenty minutes the driver watches from the passenger seat, with all the appearances of a man who lives for Cub Scout soccer. On an impulse, one sodden father walks over and chats to him, comes away with a scrap of pencilled paper.

"Who's that in't car mister?"

It is Billy Bremner, on his way to play Crystal Palace. Nothing sums up Leeds football fever more than a Scottish international who will stop "to watch the boys boot the ball about the park a wee bit". On the pitch the boys are torn between zipping through the opposition like the great Billy himself and running over to the sideline to get a mate over to that car for an autograph. In time, the car practically disappears under tiny fans. United, United, United.

What can you say about them that has not already been said? They are the super-athletes of the region—yards faster than most of their opponents, a match for any team in Europe. Their play is strong, physical, unrelenting in its force. As Bremner has said, you get nothing for coming second. For Leeds to lose at home has become a talking-point, it happens so rarely (at the time of writing this, only five times in two years). They are expected to excel and are driven on by a loyalty that is completely astride class or creed. For many people in Leeds itself they are the best thing that has ever happened; something truly wonderful.

Rugby League is a hard game. Cricket is a skilled game. Both are jealously guarded as being best in Yorkshire, pallid by comparison elsewhere. There are some frightening knocks given and taken in Rugby League football and there are some little men of genius who have made out of the back-play something very much like poetry. The game has a forcefulness and physicality that goes down well with its supporters: but by comparison with these lads,

the Leeds United team are in a class apart. Analysed, the professional skills of a top-class soccer player are sophisticated beyond
any meaningful comparison with another sport. With Leeds
United, we are talking about eleven internationals—the entire
first team has done international duty. Each individual player runs
faster, jumps higher, thinks quicker, plays harder than his
opponent.

It is their sheer athleticism that impresses itself on the mind to
begin with. That is something television coverage can never
convey about soccer; you have to watch them live to be astonished
at the diversity of their physical skills. Even for fans who would
be satisfied with a Leeds goal if it was thrown into the net by a
silly girl in bloomers, the razor-sharp quality of physical fitness
must strike an unconscious bell with a deafening ring.

The other abiding impression you take away from the match is
the extraordinary quality of team play. Whole books and many
thousands of words have been written on this aspect of United—
the relationship between the manager Don Revie, the trainer Les
Cocker, and the team itself. We shall come on to that in a moment.
But there is one other relationship to discuss, which is that
between the club and the city itself.

There are areas of England which have had football madness for
longer than Leeds. Liverpool is one; Newcastle is another. They
have been football daft round the Arsenal ground since the Alex
James days. Neither can Leeds claim the most persistently loyal
fans. Few cities in England have had an earnest injunction from
their Lord Mayor to watch more matches and raise the home
gate—as has happened when Alderman John Rafferty wore the
Lord Mayor's chain of office. The actual quality of support has
sometimes fallen short of adulation. It might even be claimed that
Leeds United has had an apathetic following—certainly at one
stage the club management itself so hinted.

There may be a simple explanation. It may be that Leeds was
and is one of the first English club sides to reproduce the merits of
the national team as directed by Sir Alf Ramsey. The style of that
play is not particularly spectacular, neither does it merit the
adjective dazzling. Ramsey and Revie (who appear to have great
respect for each other) are not the great charismatic characters of
football management. They are not the genial, fatherly types

beloved by schoolboys' comics—the sort of man who quickly plays a lad of sixteen in the all-important Cup-tie against Coke-town Rovers. They are not even especially lovable, as public figures. But—and this is the point—both men are dedicated to the ideal of team play, an ideal in which the individual willingly moulds his personality to that of the group. In this way Leeds United is first and foremost an eleven. It is a team which has no great 'characters' in it, no special favourites and no outstanding individuals.

The absence of these newsworthy qualities troubled the Press no end when Leeds first started making the headlines. It seemed, in the stylish, flippant 'sixties that without these things, football was pretty dull stuff. By the side of some other, more glamorous, less successful sides, Leeds looked an unsmiling lot. What is more, there existed in the players a kind of loyalty to the club (in effect, to Revie) that cheated the men of the Press of the rifts, rows, scandals and surprises that make up a good deal of football news. The Yorkshire talent for secretive virtue has never been more ably metaphorized than the rise to power of Leeds United. The pride they excite in the city is, by Merseyside or Teesside standards, quiet. The supporters of Leeds United have a set of values which Revie has taught them which are way in advance of their time, and may presage a sort of superstar football such as we have never seen before. The tennis critics would say that it presages nothing more than a new era of super-efficient dullness to replace the old kick-and-rush.

Life however has a nasty habit of compromising a glib genera-lization with some nubbly, indigestible pieces of news. On Black Saturday, 13th February 1971, a group of children in a pit-village between Leeds and Selby were rehearsing a pantomime to go on the following week. By its own admission this village is football-daft, with a cracking good team of its own but total football loyalty to United. The white blue and gold Leeds scarf is standard neckwear for teenage girls. The smallest tot can recite the Christian names of the team in solemn litany. Today is the last rehearsal of the panto, but it is also Cup day.

Half-way through the rehearsal a young boy rushes in and shouts "Leeds are losing at Colchester, two to nothing!" He is shouted down for pulling legs. "Nay, I'll bet you a quid. Our

dad's just come off shift and I told *him*. I wouldn't chance it there
if it weren't true." Complete pandemonium. He has found the
way to convince his mates. Nobody would tell their dad something as awful as that, not when he had just walked up from pit.
As if in sympathy, the skies blacken and the rain turns to snow.
There is worse to come. Leeds go three down. It is terrible, the
way bad news travels.

On the day that Leeds played their fifth-round tie at Colchester,
the Northern club was top of the first division, Colchester was
seventy-four places lower. Bremner was out with leg injuries but
as Friday's *Yorkshire Evening Post* put it: "To a man United are all
seasoned, experienced players and I am sure that they will cope
with gallant little Colchester's bid from the depths of the fourth
division, however frantically it may be made." Oh dear. United
pulled two goals back and lost 2–3. Colchester had played coolly
and calmly. All the frenzy was back in Leeds.

United have a special claim on the loyalty of fans in an age of
super-sport. Since their return to the first division they have twice
been beaten Cup Finalists. (The last Yorkshire Club to win at
Wembley was Sheffield Wednesday. That was in 1935.) Their
European record has been excellent and their League play has
been openly copied by less successful clubs. Only Leeds fans
could say, with complete conviction, that they would not have
George Best in the side not even if *he* paid *them*. The Colchester
defeat was in this context. Taken out of proportion it was a blow
to something more than football form. In its context it was
simply the price of excellence. By agreement among almost
all sports writers, 'gallant little Colchester' played better and won
deservedly. For ninety minutes in a season of over sixty matches,
working six days a week with a dedication shared by only a few
athletes, Leeds stumbled. It happens every other week in English
football. In Leeds, it was almost unbelievable.

"Me dad's taken me mam to Pontefract for t'shopping," a
little girl says tearfully as the panto rehearsal packs up. "He'll play
pop when he finds out, he will that!" She sums it all up. There will
be that kind of pop played in every pub in the three Ridings
tonight—especially in Hull, who beat Brentford at home and are
the only surviving Yorkshire club in the competition.

XII

SHOPS

WHERE does Leeds shop? The city prides itself on being the best shopping centre in Yorkshire. Certainly if you live in Ripon, they will advise unblinkingly to go to Harrogate for what they do not stock or cannot be bothered to order. That is the way of a rural town. In Harrogate which has its own pride (it once *described itself* as the most snobbish town in Yorkshire) they will probably wrestle with you a bit before admitting that you may do better in Leeds. So far as Leeds is concerned it is *the* regional shopping centre, no argument. You might go to Dewsbury market for your cloth or York for your books. They say that Harrogate is not too snobbish to take your money for things like antiques. But for the biggest displays and the most choice, Leeds is best for most things. It must infuriate Sheffield.

In the motorway age that the city so desperately longs to help into being, a slight word of caution might be entered. Although Leeds has variety and glamour, when it is as easy for the many to drive to Manchester or Sheffield, York or Doncaster as it is already becoming for the few, Leeds might live to rue its easy acknowledgement that it is first in a novice race.

With a remarkable flash of genius, the city fathers have latched on to this danger. The city has proposals to create what will be the biggest pedestrian precinct in Europe. A start has already been made, with great success. The full extension of the idea could make Leeds into one of the most pleasant city centres of its size in Britain and that not only for shopping purposes.

The first new shopping precinct was created just in time for Christmas 1970. It was part of the central area master plan which was in turn a division of the overall development plan for the city. Put simply, three congested streets, Bond Street, Commercial Street and Lands Lane were denied to traffic and paved over.

There are attractive details in the scheme but in essence it had a simplicity which must make former councils wonder why they had not thought of it before.

No property was acquired by the city along the route of this precinct. None was needed. The whole of the new is in plan, not elevation, and therefore fairly unobtrusive. All the original elevations are retained. It is this that makes the precinct so interesting. The three streets it affected in the first phase were bisecting a rectangular block of nineteenth-century building in the old heart's core of Leeds. In its day, this area had become a shambles of very mixed housing and services, gradually sorting itself into some kind of propriety. At the top end the new precinct links Schofield's, one of the biggest stores in Leeds, with Thornton's and Queen's Arcades, which have some of the smaller shops and services in the city centre. Schofield's fronts the Headrow and is a 'thirties development. It would not disgrace Oxford Street. The two arcades are as Northern as brass-band music. Before Land's Lane was paved over the two styles were separate and remote. They now merge in a really interesting way.

When the last car passed through the area, shoppers' normal sight-line, which was depressed to meet the eye of oncoming traffic, was raised and allowed to wander. Leeds suddenly discovered that Land's Lane was quite an interesting place. For example there is a huge bay window rising above a baker's which has been completely forgotten for generations. It can now be seen as an interesting architectural detail, an oddity that is both funny and attractive. The light reflected from the shoe-shop right at the bottom of the Lane strikes up the precinct in a manner never before studied; and so on. The city architect, Mr. C. W. Stanley, might himself have been surprised by similar details which came to light.

The most pleasant thing about the scheme has been its retention of the nineteenth-century character of the streets as such. By leaving the elevations alone, the grand canyon effect of some other cities' solution to shopping problems has been avoided. Shoppers like it, and the trading potential has risen sharply. As an unexpected piece of conservation it has had nothing but praise.

The same treatment cries out to be done on the eastern side

of Briggate, between it and Vicar Lane. There already exist four arcades. At the bottom of the hill it is a short step away to the covered market. New plans have been put to council to extend the pedestrian precinct throughout this area too, closing Kirkgate, King Edward Street and Queen Victoria Street. When these are paved over something might happen that has been unable to happen yet.

We have seen time and again how Briggate is the key to Leeds history. On that short hill much of Leeds has been made and lost. It is a wide and extremely busy roadway today and it emphasizes an old division in the city. Westwards of Briggate is the traditional old town. The shopping precinct we have discussed is known locally as the Golden Square Mile. It is located at the very heart of business in Leeds for 200 years.

East of Briggate has a different shopping character altogether. Eastern development from the Briggate area was always slower. In 1819, Bilham explains, "not a single manufacture is to be found more than one mile east or north of Leeds". Leeds was traditionally a left-handed city, taking Briggate as its trunk. If the great benefit of the shopping precinct in the Golden Square Mile takes root as firmly in the east side of Briggate, an old class division will disappear.

The fronting shops and stores to Briggate are in the big city idiom, but between them and Vicar Lane are a host of smaller properties whose speciality is in cheap articles. In a few cases the goods are both cheap and nasty and although it is hard to prove, the subjective impression is that Briggate holds back shoppers in this area of Leeds from a foray into better-class shops and stores. By the same token nobody with a credit account at Schofield's would start their Saturday afternoon out at the Vicar Lane shops (although to be scrupulously fair in this, they might land up there).

Central Leeds has been cheated of a large-scale architectural centre such as a Broderick would have provided, given half the chance. The new precincts will give to the common streets something of the pleasure and peacefulness of a vast square, but with an additional purpose. In fact, the precincts will do better than large-scale civic squares, which in the glorious illogic of English life become mere roundabouts in any case. They will open up the entire central area to the enquiring eye, and make Leeds worth a visit not only as a showcase for retail goods, but also as a great city in the image of its nineteenth-century origins. If at the same time the 'west' and 'east' of Leeds are laid to rest and the place learns to become ambidextrous, that will be no bad thing. And if the cheap and nasty face their real competition, it is just possible that wholly new and unexpected shops will force their way in. We could have one day an arcade of books, stamps, toys, models, records, games, or a street of swinging boutiques. We could even have the first Latin quarter north of Soho: but perhaps that is asking too much, even of Project Leeds.

The outer circumference of the new precinct is bounded by Boar Lane, Briggate and the Headrow. (One side of the rectangle abuts the banking and commercial centre of Leeds, of which more in its place.) Probably the multiple store with most claim on Leeds loyalty is Marks and Spencer, for it was in Leeds market that the vast trading empire started. From a penny-bazaar stall to the Marks and Spencer Corporation is a giant growth. Some of the original personalized trading custom persists—for example, Marks and Spencer's policy is always to replace faulty goods without question. It has actually happened in Leeds that one of the original stall-girls in Mr. Marks's Bazaar has had a handbag sold to her with a defective zip. She took it back, waved it in the manager's face and told him straight that Mr. Marks would be ashamed if he could see the way the stall had turned out.

There are of course a number of big retail stores in the city. Schofield's, which we have already mentioned, is a family store with roots in the city. Across the Headrow is Lewis's, part of the Lewis partnership chain; just as Mathias Robinson in Briggate is a part of Debenham's group of companies. In Albion Street, Leeds has one of the biggest co-operative stores ever founded in the North of England. But of course the shops which have the greatest connection with Leeds are the multiple-store tailors. Mass-produced clothes are an invention of Leeds business and the city is ringed by the tailoring firms whose Leeds factories supply the whole country with household names.

At the western end of the Headrow is the monument to a revolution in clothing, Barran's original factory. It was Barran who, with the help of a Jewish veneer-cutter, developed a method of cutting many copies of a pattern in one operation, just as a woodworker would jig-cut identical veneer shapes. By breaking down the essential manufacture of a garment into single pieces, and by producing these in great quantity, Barran was able to use the power of the sewing-machine to tailor ready-made clothing in the mass.

The factory manufacture of clothing and its associated spin-off, gave rise to multi-million-pound industrial operations which has had an effect on the whole country. The brilliant lead in marketing which Marks and Spencer showed the world has made this effect so commonplace as to be almost invisible. Marks and Spencer do not themselves manufacture a single item: they specify to eager manufacturers a close description of an article they wish to sell. The size of the potential order is so enormous that the retailing firm can create its own standard of quality at the planning stage, before a line of production has been commenced. Marks and Spencer are in this way the most successful marketing organization ever created in this country, earnestly copied by their competitors and associates. When they say that almost every woman in the country is wearing some item of their underwear, it is a sort of metaphor for the invisible revolution in clothing standards—and fashions—that began in Leeds and has now become world wide.

It is a curious reflection that the best of Leeds style may be next to the skin. Mass-produced clothing is by itself only a logical extension of the factory system of making cloth. Mass retailing, with all its sophistications of sizing, patterns, colours and materials is the next logical step in that chain. But without the sort of commercial acumen that started it off in Leeds, and gave in time a style to a nation, mass-produced clothes could look as they were reputed to look behind the Iron Curtain and in Russia until recently—civilian uniforms. The other half of the folk myth that all the women in Britain buy their undies at 'Marks and Sparks' is the story that the managers of the firm are forced to create local stock differences in different areas, so that their women customers are not all wearing the same colour pants. Certainly when school children debate the motion "That Marks and Spencer has done more than Marx and Engels for the people of their country" the young Marxists must squirm in their St. Michael's socks as they hammer home the argument.

Market trading on Saturday morning

In the part of Leeds to the north of the Headrow, between it and the city's colleges complex, is the Merrion Centre. The basis of this development is a shopping precinct incorporating an hotel, office accommodation, a cinema, two discothèques, a bowling alley, dance hall and covered market. There was even a moving pavement to carry you up to the piped music and the shopping parade. Leeds folk do not seem to be averse to music, for that has stayed: the moving pavement stopped shortly after it started and has not resumed.

The Merrion Centre is a commercial development which has not seemed entirely to have met Leeds squarely face to face, although it may take time for new patterns in shopping to establish themselves. Leeds is an interesting example of a shopping population which favours multiple choice. Despite the giant combines, Leeds is loaded with small businesses and modest concessionaires. The people seem to like shopping in the way that all big cities shop: they shop around. Choice means what it says. For example many small tailoring manufacturers exist along the big ones, and many bespoke tailors alongside them. From a shopper's point of view there is nothing to be taken for granted in the claims of the big stores, or the chain shops. The great mass of shopping is firmly at the city centre, with some notable exceptions. The Arndale Development Trust is a Yorkshire company and was responsible for the rejuvenation of Headingley as a shopping area. In Headingley it has provided, along with a modern site for big and small retailers, a rooftop car-park which is the only practicable form of off-street parking in this crowded suburb. In Crossgates, Arndale have gone one better with an immensely popular shopping precinct on a site already five miles from the city square. 'The Arndale' at Crossgates has a dog-leg pedestrian avenue built through it that is completely weatherproof and links the full range of shopping services with ample parking provision.

The municipal precinct in the Golden Square Mile will complete a repatterning of retail trading which is all very recent in time. The look and feel of Leeds shops was, ten years ago, limited to their proximity or otherwise to the Headrow. New developments have made for much fiercer competition and more streamlined and attacking policies. But there is a resistance to

10

The City Hall and Town Hall

conformity about the Leeds character that may slow down the more aggressive speculators. Leeds shoppers are notoriously difficult to please and prudent in their spending habits. Metropolitan London would find some of their taste—in furniture and furnishings for example—pretty desperate and might consider their general outlook a niggardly one. It may be so. But anyone who has been to London will reflect on return that in one area at least Leeds still leads. The city has some of the best-dressed girls in Britain. This may also apply to the men; but the girls, so to speak, stand out more.

XIII

PLEASURES

LEEDS pubs can have a shattering effect on Southerners, used to the small bars and Tudor snugs of the Home Counties. They go in for size in Leeds and they go to a pub to drink. The sort of folk-museum decorations beloved by some brewers' architects are mercifully rare. A Leeds pub must have character and atmosphere from the people who use it, without the addition of fancy wallpapers and mock-oak beams. Some of the bigger pubs—like the 'Fforde Greene' in Roundhay Road—are awesome in their size and raw functionalism.

At one time Briggate was full of great coaching inns, three of the best on the right-hand side of the road, where the big chain stores are now. On the left-hand side of Briggate, Thornton's Arcade and Queen's Arcade were made from the coach yards of the 'Talbot' and 'Rose and Crown'. We can get an idea of the shape of these yards from one of the smaller ones that is still there. On the same side of Briggate in its own yard is the 'Ship Inn'. 'The Ship' was one of the lesser coaching inns, from which *Accommodation* and later on *True Briton* ran to Wakefield. By comparison with some of the other undertakings, this was a local run. 'The White Horse' in Boar Lane, opposite Holy Trinity Church, and 'The Bull and Mouth', more or less where Woolworth's now stands in Briggate, were mighty inns in the heyday of coaching. In 1838, before the new railway plunged all into darkness, 130 coaches ran to and from Leeds daily, the earliest mail setting off at three in the morning, the latest passenger leaving at ten driving through the Clevelands overnight to Redcar.

'The Old White Horse' was pulled down when Boar Lane was widened. From 1792 it had gradually worked up a big business in coaching. From the early days when the booking office was in an oyster bar down the street it became in time a good-class hotel

147

with excellent coaching connections to all parts. On the King's birthday, 1809, the *London Union* commenced its run from there to London, which it completed in thirty-six gruelling hours. Coaches came to leave for Manchester, Kendal, Scarborough, Ripon and Harrogate, with bread and butter runs to catch the steamers at Selby and Castleford.

'The Bull and Mouth' was still in Briggate at the end of the last century, its cellar stables filled with the junk of an honoured coaching pub. The man generally reckoned to be king of the coaching business was Mathew Ousthwaite, who had the good sense to concentrate his attention on the horses and leave the running of the pubs to landlords. Ousthwaite had stabling in most Leeds inns and was actually competing with himself so far as routes and timetables were concerned. In his day, he had 200 horses going for him, but by 1840 the railway had taken away his trade. The romance of names like *True Briton*, *Tantivy*, *Perseverance* and *Eclipse* passed to the steam engine. As for the horses they turned with their owner to the more prosaic business of general carting.

Probably the best-known city-centre pub in Leeds is 'Whitelock's Turk's Head Tavern', which is in a ginnel (alley) off Briggate. Whitelock's is a long narrow pub, hardly wider than an average-size sitting-room and almost invariably crammed to the doors. It is miraculously preserved as a nineteenth-century 'luncheon bar', with good brass rails, copper-sheeted tables, fine glass and mirrors. At one end you can buy the sandwich of your choice, pointing to what filling you want from a great array of possibilities. Red cabbage, pickled walnuts, fresh sliced onions and the rest to tempt you here. At the other end is the popular diner, where the speciality is a plate of whitebait taken before tackling the prime beef. Whitelock's has an enviable casualness born of sublime self-confidence. In the summer months the overflow from the pub will drink outside in an alley most Southern landlords would use to store their empty crates. Thin sinuous girls have a decided advantage in getting near enough the bar to order. Solid bulky citizens arrive early and stay late.

Behind the town hall is 'The Victoria', a pub with a long bar overlooked by the Queen-Empress in widow's weeds. 'The Victoria' has several quite different clienteles. Close by are the hospitals and magistrates' courts, whose staff (and clients) mix with painters, sculptors and their students. In the evening 'The Victoria' has its quiet hour when the locals stop by on their way home from work, followed later on still by an invasion from the town hall entertainment for the night—rock concert, Halle visit or wrestling match. It is a restless, energetic, no-nonsense pub that is well worth your visit.

'The Coburg', at the top of Cookridge Street, is the poly-technic's pub. A little to the north along Woodhouse Lane is 'The Fenton', a pub which has long been a friend to the BBC across the road. 'The Fenton' had a fantastic period of life when the inner ring road was being built. The lads—many of them Jocks—who built that, used to call in for a lunchtime chat with actresses and writers who were making the BBC North Region a by-word for enterprising drama productions. One bar of 'The Fenton' was eventually called Studio Six, in honour of the great work done there by the more public-spirited BBC staff. Higher up Woodhouse Lane, opposite the university, 'The Eldon' has performed a similar function. 'The Eldon' is a poet's pub, and more than one university tutorial has been conducted there.

There is a pub in Leeds for every kind of drinker, with every kind of side interest. Tetley's is the name of the ale, and you can practically throw a stone on the roof of the brewery from most pub steps. Tetley's is held by some incomers to be an acquired taste. In Leeds it is almost a test of loyalty to like the local ale. It is at the least tactful to say there is nothing quite like it anywhere, but a real Leeds loiner will go further, much further.

Two Leeds United supporters go to London for an away match. They spend all night looking for a Tetley's house in Soho. At last, in a back ginnel reminiscent of home, they find an obscure little pub with the familiar huntsman sign of the Tetley Brewery swinging outside. Relieved beyond measure, they stagger in and order two pints of Guinness.

A couple of dozen stalwarts gather in a Hunslet pub. The Leeds Arts Lab comes into existence whenever these faithful gather together: tonight a specially invited group from London are performing. Lots of black sweaters and earnest chat from the guests, who go through a well-practised routine with enormous professionalism, considering the miserable surroundings. Groovy things can seldom have happened in less promising circumstances it would appear; but everything is listened to with great attention and respect (so much so that even the most obvious jokes are missed in the cathedral quiet).

The Arts Lab is a very remarkable institution indeed, the more so because it asks nothing from the world on the way to do its thing. The audience, which is also pretty well the membership, is young, alert and excessively polite and patient. If the licensee has let them in for the sake of the drink they might consume, he's a disappointed man. (In actual fact, this is the reverse of the case: the brewery as well as the licensee are patient and sympathetic towards the idea.) The evening is well-organized, enjoyable and nicely cool. The organizers are not students but young workers and their girls who simply want to make new scenes. As they troop out into a cold, dank fog rising off the river, nobody in the downstairs bars bats an eyelid. It's a sort of hand-rolled entertainment-cum-belief that sends strangers away greatly impressed. The lab goes bust and comes on hard again with a fitful, flickering kind of energy that is all the more attractive because of the hard, brash, unrelenting lights of the things it is fighting.

Leeds Town Hall, the night of the big, big concert. Against the backdrop of the benches which lead up to the organ there is the daunting spectacle of loudspeakers piled one on top of another like luggage in a porters' strike at City Station. The people who sit nearest this wall of speakers are brave indeed. When their mums and dads come in here for wrestling or the stamp exhibition, or the charity bazaar, or the Philharmonic, they can have no idea of the solid chunks of sound hurled around at a progressive rock concert. Busy lads in cyclamen-coloured shirts and tan suits leap around fiddling with the amplifiers—the road-managers and the engineers and the just plain nervous. Behind the stand the groupie girls sit out on their own, looking and maybe feeling acutely self-conscious. The concert is late in starting and goes on to be very late in starting. Nobody minds. Nobody even notices. The preparatory rites with the amplifiers, the mike-stands and the speakers are solemn enough spectacle.

The natural acoustic of Broderick's Main Hall has given

pleasure to thousands. The International Pianoforte competitions are heard here, the lightest notes moving in clear air, each separate part of an arpeggio distinct and sharp. The Concert Hall has accommodated a choir of 700 children and many distinguished musicians have played within its rather plain walls. The Concert Hall is not acclaimed as a miracle of acoustics but it has not disgraced its architect either. The noise we are going to hear now is almost to baffle description.

It is sound raised to the level where it touches not just the ear but the entire skin surface. The hands and face seem to act as receivers, sound driving through in invisible shocks that create a genuine psychological disturbance. Saying that the sound is deafening is a pallid way of putting things: it fills the ear like a hardpacked snowball, or a blizzard of freezing wind. The mind struggles to find adequate metaphors: *no* sound could be this loud and penetrating, the mind says, as the watering eyes goggle at the lads in cyclamen and tan as they try to wrestle another decibel from the gear. A number from this group is like suffering severe exposure on a mountainside. The whole body is flayed alive. When the silence at last comes, the audience greets it in amazed respect, the sort of respect reserved for someone you thought was dead, but it turns out isn't. Such is the physical presence of the silence that people are embarrassed and do not know what to say. A twitching dee-jay says it for them, with a reverential awe all his own. "That, my friends," he says, "was just too much, too much, baby."

The Radio Leeds studios are on the east side of the Merrion Centre development. Almost opposite its doors and apparently dumped down on the pavement is a polyhedral of a pub called 'The General Wade'. At a quarter to six in Radio Leeds the foyer and reception desk is completely deserted as if some urgent intelligence has come in from the agencies and the station manager has called his staff together for an agonized conference. A small queue of mild, shy men gather with only the station budgie for company. From time to time a shirtsleeved reporter zooms into the main editorial space, only to leave again at double the speed.

The editorial work of the station is done in a large open-plan office crammed with desks, papers, telephones and people. The atmosphere is cheerful and just a fraction lunatic. Nobody quite knows where anyone else is, but will fling themselves out to look with all the energy of keen footballers trying for a place in the first team. When the reception desk is deserted, you are trusted not to steal a studio but wait around for action. Radio Leeds has built itself on a determination to be a community radio. The spirit of the main office is the spirit of the broadcasts themselves—friendly in a schoolboyish kind of way. Speed lends importance to every action. Telephones are snatched up with an urgency that would do credit to any kidnap victim. Wild whoops of dismay or victory fill the air over the unrelenting chatter of typewriters. Whatever else Leeds expected from its local radio it was not this ceaseless drum of enthusiasm. Radio Leeds is competing with a very large evening newspaper that goes out in two editions (three on Saturdays). It started life with a good few technical problems of reception but a much more important communication difficulty that the monster *Yorkshire Evening Post* posed it. People were extremely dubious about the value of Radio Leeds when it started out—and it is still studiously ignored by influential sectors of Leeds life. Its answer to that has been to get happy, and stay that way.

The shy little group of men waiting with the budgie are rescued by a pretty girl and introduced to a cheerfully flustered producer. They are joining him in forming a discussion prog-ramme immediately after the local news. The producer explains how he will open and close the show (and at this word half his parcel of experts winces); demands that no one bangs the table to emphasize a point, or kick the floor in nerves or exasperation; and then leads the way on tiptoe into the studio, where the news-caster raises a solemn hand in welcome while in the middle of describing a warehouse fire.

Local radio *is* local. The interesting quality it has, and the job it does best, is in just that area which would appear to be its weakest point—newsgathering and background features. Com-mercial radio could never bother itself with the detail of local life that a station like Radio Leeds digs out. Nor would commercial radio encourage the community to make use of its broadcasting facility in quite the way the BBC monopoly allows. Critics can point to some stretches of local radio which are little more than talking newspapers; and by the standards of the BBC main services, local radio anywhere is a mess. In its three years of existence however, it has established an alternative to national and regional broadcasting that has released some powerful energies.

Our panel of experts seat themselves with elaborate care round a circular table. A microphone is fixed in the middle. Taking care not so much as to touch the table with a stray fingertip they wait, feet firmly anchored to the studio floor. Then, as the producer accepts his cue and leads in the programme, all four pull out streams of rustling paper and find an irresistable desire to cough. The Radio Leeds man does not falter for a second, but puts his fingers to his lips, then throws the gesture away with a wave of the wrist. He leads them in gently but firmly to what they know, what they are good at. The discussion gets under way.

Outside, in 'The General Wade', the journalist who reads the news eats a sandwich and sips his beer hastily. At six-thirty he is going to record a vicar on vandalism in churches. Then there is the housewife who has written some stories for children, followed by an outside broadcast at a working men's club. At Radio Leeds only the budgie sits tight.

Leeds is proud of the attention it is getting from town-planning and traffic experts for its attempts to avoid strangulation. It would be stretching a point to say that it was a pleasure to drive in Leeds, but the situation is helped by two remarkable pioneering city-centre roads.

The Upperhead Row and Lowerhead Row are shown on the first Leeds map of 1560. The 'head' they relate to is of course the head of Briggate, the brow of its long hill up from the river. As the town grew older, these streets became built up on both sides, forming a narrow, mean, congested thoroughfare. The architecture of these shops and offices was nothing very special either. We have already seen how the town has chased its own tail for a true centre, a central point of comfort round which it can curl. From the crossroads formed by Briggate and the Headrows in the early years of this century, the town hall was hardly visible. The parish church was out of sight, and so was the City Square. Yet here, at this particular crossroads, was the crux of Leeds as a shopping centre.

In the early years of 1930, Leeds astonished and delighted the rest of the country by taking on one of the biggest city re-developments at one of the worst of times. The two Headrows were unified as one double-carriageway with a centre refuge. More importantly, the whole of the north side from Quarry Hill to the town hall was demolished. A new façade was offered for the whole length. The key to this new style was the million-pound Lewis's built at the intersection with Briggate.

The new Headrow let light in, in much the same way that the University redevelopment let in not merely the light of know-ledge, but the long afternoon sun. Leeds would be memorable to a casual visitor for nothing else but its Headrow, so striking is the effect of this double road cut through the centre of the city. The architecture of the new northern façade will never excite the envy of future generations. At the same time, its light stone suggest modernity, of a kind. The ambiguity that surrounds Leeds's character is strong here: the scale of the Headrow is almost Roman and the buildings strong and masculine in style. The old sentimentality of landmarks like Merryboys Hill have been smoothed away to a dip in the road before it crosses Cookridge Street. The Headrow suggests power, but of a kind that one cannot quite name.

In the post-war years, the roadway was extended past the town hall and terminated by a huge roundabout, flanked by police headquarters and the telephone exchange. Inevitably it became a speed route through Leeds from the westerly towns, so that at times in the early 'sixties it could appear that the whole of Bradford was being dismantled and driven on lorries through the heart of Leeds. To cross the Headrow on foot was like jumping into the Western Avenue or, more appropriately, taking on Oxford Street in London.

The solution was bold and adventurous. The city set about building an inner ring road roughly parallel with the Headrow, this time avoiding the problems of an open road by plunging the traffic into cuttings and tunnels. Westbound traffic can now zip through the city in uninterrupted streams and connect with the road to York and the A1. The deep trench of the main route is connected by curving feeder lanes to the other points of the compass. There is a kind of elegance about this massive piece of civil engineering and when complete there may even be some delicacy. The inner ring road assumes the domination of the motor-car and has been criticized for just that assumption, its critics suggesting that it might have been better to plan for an environment at the centre that denies access altogether to cars. At present the inner ring road is lightly used, by comparison with what volume of traffic it could take. It may be that discouragements to motorists will in time result in no more than the present traffic flow along its route. In which case the system will justify itself.

The worst that could happen is that traffic density would build up until a perpetual antlike stream of traffic curved round the feeders or flew along the straights. Then Leeds might become a victim of its own ingenuity. Having done it once, the temptation might be there to do it again, with further massive concessions to the car, a whole new network of sunken roads and their accelerator lanes. But at present, the inner ring road is one of the minor pleasures of the city. Vastly less confusing than the tight little battle for space in Bradford, less terrifying than the brutal, mean structures of a city like Birmingham, Leeds manages to be that rare thing, a city centre you can drive through in two minutes. That must be some kind of tribute, however double-edged.

Roundhay Park on Boxing Day. For the past two years there has been more than enough snow to fulfil that dream of England, a white Christmas. At the bottom of a natural amphitheatre the cricket table is covered in snow and the slopes leading down to it are buzzing with children, sledges, dogs and the occasional self-conscious man on skis. The snow transforms not only the landscape but the figures in it. It should snow like this every Boxing Day, for the effect it has on the sledgers.

Roundhay Park is one of the great unsung beauties of Leeds. In 1818 Mr. Thomas Nicholson had a house built for him by Clark of York at the crest of a long eastward-facing slope. This house looked out on to grounds which had already seen the hand of a born improver, in the old tradition of improving property owners. Wike Beck ran through Nicholson's property. At the time of the Napoleonic Wars, which was a time of acute depression, he caused a quarry on his lands to be transformed into a lake

—Waterloo Lake, a fine title for a lake anywhere but a triumphant clarion to the men who made this one. Roundhay had as much in common with the muddy crossroads about Quatre Bras as Nicholson had with Napoleon. The land is hilly, subtle, complicated by plantings of trees, artificial vistas, corners of secrecy, exclamation marks of Victorian bandstands and follies. In the snow it is all exquisite.

The city acquired the Nicholson estate in 1872 and paid £139,000 for the massive parklands. It was money well spent. At the western end a nine-hole golf course, at the eastern end an open-air swimming pool and in between as pleasant and rural a walk as you will find anywhere. There is a children's boating lake, where the model power-boat enthusiasts have their sway on Sundays. On the big lake there is enough water for several hundred fishermen and large Edwardian rowing boats to row out over the deepest parts, which are said to be of incredible depths. Just how deep Waterloo Lake is, and just what is lost or dumped within it are topics of conversation all over Leeds, not merely among the middle-class children who live round about. Roundhay Park is that rare piece of England, a public property that has the public esteem. Considering the heavy traffic it gets, it is a remarkably clean and unlittered environment. Its successful management and the similar efficiency shown everywhere there is a bit of grass and woodland in Leeds has made the Public Parks Department one of the most well known in the country.

It is of course a popular venue for all sorts of occasions. There are extensive football pitches and cricket tables, donkey rides in summer, a permanent fairground for small children and tom-tiddlers' grounds all along the ravine cut by the beck. It is a spell of countryside in the middle of some of the densest population in Britain. In the summer there is the Printers' Gala to capture the thousands, with cycling, athletics, sideshows and all the fun of the fair. You could lose a couple of thousand people in Roundhay Park and not disturb its calm by a jot.

Every Saturday and Sunday, the whole year round, a significant part of Leeds life takes itself off to the countryside. Incomers to Yorkshire explain this phenomenon in different ways. There is the argument that the cities are so ugly and depressing that people are forced to leave them whenever they can for the sake of health and sanity. Another explanation is that suburban Yorkshire loves its motor-car and has a blind urge to drive it somewhere picturesque. Some cynics suggest that it is in the character of Yorkshiremen to look for something that isn't there, and this explains the attraction of the empty spaces.

None of these explanations satisfy the facts. Yorkshire is the largest county in England, with some of the most austerely beautiful scenery to be found anywhere. From the Cleveland Hills, where the old Drover's Road rose on its way to York, the industrial West Riding is nothing but a faint smudge of blue on the horizon. From a glider circling above Sutton Bank, any observer would take this county for what it is, a massive complex of open and dramatic countryside—the traditional 'rolling acres' of Yorkshire.

In the Pennine Dales, industrial Yorkshire is a similarly distant thunder. The people there live close to the seasons, knowing when to plant and when to reap by the experience passed to them by their parents, who learned it themselves from men and women who hardly knew the fate of their own generation in the mill towns. The Dales and the North York Moors are separated by the great, generous, calm Vale of York, where the same story holds good.

Much of Yorkshire's rural charm is secretive, a quality of landscape which is perhaps induced in its people. Certainly there is more respect for the rural worker and less contempt or indifference from his city brother. Only a Londoner would describe a farm labourer as 'a swede': in Yorkshire there is a general sense of loyalty to the soil—and to animals—which is remarkable. The common Yorkshire word 'folk' is extended to city-dweller and village labourer alike. Pithy country humour, with its suggestion of native wisdom is extremely popular. The correspondence pages of the city's paper attest to its efficacy as the salt of everyday experience.

It follows that Yorkshire people have a love of the countryside that is by any standards truly phenomenal. In this, the man from the Dewsbury Road, or Halton, in Leeds, has as much to offer as his distant relative who actually lives in the Dales. Neither is this love at all sentimental or passive. Leeds knows as much about

its surrounding countryside as most public commissions of
enquiry, for there is a tradition of amateur interest that is a vital
part of the region's character. Furthermore, countryside amenities
are used and enjoyed for all they are worth. Inside every Yorkshireman is a rambler trying to get out.

The Ramblers' Association probably heads the list of societies
whose watchdog activities ensure the safety of rural amenities.
It has proliferated committees to deal with almost every aspect
of the countryside and commands the sort of official respect that
it deserves. Rambling goes with Yorkshiremen as fitly as bacon
with eggs—all ages enjoy it and one of the common sights on
any piece of open country is to see a small party of men and women
with rucksack, boots and turned-down stockings walking
the roads and fields of their native county. People fall in love, get
engaged and in the fullness of time die in their Sunday ramble;
if they also conceived their children and brought them into the
world in the green fields it would not be unfitting.

As well as the almost religious joy in nature and natural things,
a Yorkshireman's love of countryside includes great scholarship.
The topography of Yorkshire has excited a body of learning that
one can describe as 'the green university', a university of knowledge and love all the more remarkable for being strictly amateur.
The green university includes in its prospectus geology, local
history, botany, ornithology, even conchology. It has produced
men of very great intellectual merit—for example, Dr. Arthur
Raistrick, who was trained as an engineer at Leeds University but
has become the doyen of many hundreds of men and women like
him, who treasure their county and study its landscape. Arthur
Raistrick's book *The Pennine Dales*, written when he was well into
his seventies, is the culmination of a lifetime of study and an
attitude of mind framed early by respect and joy. He is the sort
of authority Yorkshire loves best; and like the best, has devoted
himself to teaching several generations of fellow ramblers.

The countryside and the city are hard by each other in Yorkshire. It would be an unusual man in Leeds who could not take
you a walk in the Dales, show you a nest, or a ruined castle, or an
old pack road, or a particular plant, and find you a favourite spot
for a picnic. Canoeing, sailing, gliding, walking or climbing,
Leeds goes back to the Dales countryside as a Londoner might go

to the seaside. When he is there, he is knowledgeable (and some-times intrepid) in a way that puts some other cities to shame. It is a kind of honour with him to know and to guard. It is something completely unexpected in the context of the workaday city he has built for himself.

XIV

LEEDS AND REGION

Leeds is joined at its western edges to Bradford. The local government boundaries conflict with the telephone region, the bus services tangle. The two cities are nine miles apart from centre to centre, but have swollen in time to touch each other at their boundaries. To the south lie the independent townships with a history of their own, owing allegiance to neither giant. But between Leeds and Bradford the shading off from one place to another is fine indeed except to the jealous eye of the local man. The northern ring road is a sort of boundary mark and Pudsey the town that buffers the two restless cities. Commuter Leeds—the obvious commuter country that attracts the people who want the best of both worlds—is to the north-west and east of the city.

Until the 1870s, the private carriage and the horse-drawn coach vied with each other to link the eleven townships of Leeds which fall within the city boundary. In those days, Bradford was a couple of hours away across an obvious natural obstacle, the high ridge that separates the two places. It was not until 1871 that the local authority was made responsible for its own roadway system, an Act which had greatest effect on the roads between the towns and cities of the region. Along the route of the railways little villages had begun to put down new housing of a kind which still seems out of character with the ancient composure of the High Street—'crescents' and 'avenues' of 'villas', a whole new vocabulary of architecture tacked on to the sleepy anonymity of the original village.

Suburban Leeds was created in this period on the impetus given to development by the Tramways Act. The horse-drawn tram opened up the green fields and forgotten townships. The first horse-drawn tram ran to Headingley (still bus route No. 1) and was swiftly followed by trams to Chapeltown, Kirkstall, Hunslet

Leeds Pedestrian Precinct—Commercial Street

and Marsh Lane. The trams ran every quarter of an hour and were designed as a service to attract the greatest popular use. Meanwood and Wortley were in time added to the network. Trams stimulated housing development in Leeds in two ways. Artisans were enabled to live farther from their place of work— for example a man might now live in Meanwood and work in Hunslet, and not count it anything unusual. At the same time his boss and the clerks who had a boss's ambition could separate themselves in the place they chose to live as well as by the work they did. The tram did as much as anything to put people in their place. The two developments interacted, pushing housing further and further toward the periphery. The old Leeds about Briggate died to the solemn rattle of the horse-tram.

Trams started their life as a working-class alternative to the private carriage, but in Leeds they did a great deal to help create the better suburbs. Roundhay Park, which had been acquired by the city, opened to the public in 1872. Without the potentiality the tram brought in its path, Roundhay could have remained a virtual private park. But here was a means of transport which could take a family along in great propriety, without loss of dignity or status, to the farthest parts of the city. The average speed was six miles an hour and the fares were low. The whole thing was a progressive step of the sort that folk had known all along would follow from the concentration of so much industry and science. For those who liked their progress played to a march tune, the tram was a lively melody, all the better for being thoroughly decent.

Gentlemen sat upstairs for the convenience of smoking and manly conversation. Since the sides of the early trams were open, to reduce the overall weight, a lady could not in any case sit upstairs, because of the dangers to her 'understandings' from prying eyes. Later versions of the prototypes were fitted with 'modesty boards'. With that lovable feeling for domesticity that turned first-class railway carriages into travelling sitting-rooms, the interior of the tram was comparatively luxurious and as much like home as the proprietors could afford. The Tramways Act of 1870 had put trams in the development of private enterprise for twenty-one years. Glasgow was the first city to introduce steam in the place of horses. The Board of Trade licence insisted

11

Brodrick's Town Hall—a landmark and a milestone

on some rigorous design elements, shrouding the working parts
and reducing the noise to its minimum. The first results were
scaled-down locomotives which looked like nothing so much as a
seaside urinal on wheels. The new power-weight ratio allowed
greater freedom with the passenger car, however. Gentlemen at
last had a roof over their heads.

Leeds scored a notable first in the development of trams. In
1891 it was the first city to run electric trams by the overhead
system. This solved a lot of problems with electrification, including the accidental electrification of dogs and small boys by
inefficient conduiting in the roadway. The first overhead line in
the country ran to Roundhay. There are a few yards of the track
left there today in a side way of the terminus.

In 1894, the trams were municipalized, as had been provided for
in the earlier legislation. An electric tram was obviously the thing,
fulfilling the idea of progress in more than one way at once. The
operating costs of tramways fell sharply and the corporation was
able to force fares down to absolute minimum. The effect on
housing was commensurate. Under private ownership you could
travel 1,500 yards for a penny fare. Municipal trams increased the
same stage to two miles. There was a halfpenny stage for short
journeys and early morning concessions for workers. Cities grew
wheels. Overhead electrification proved so effective that in five
years, 1900 to 1905, sixty-one municipal authorities in Britain
started electrification schemes, although not all of them by the
overhead system. The conduit system was perfected in London,
with colossal noise at the busy junctions. The scenes at the Elephant
and Castle had to be heard to be believed as trams came crashing
round from five great roads.

In the Leeds region, trams were quickly used to connect up the
nearest towns—Morley, Stanningley, Pudsey, Horsforth, Roth-
well and Wakefield, even Guiseley. These are westerly and
southerly townships. Where the trams went, the housing sprang
up. Between Leeds and Bradford the houses were cheap and not
very exciting; but, as we have seen, trams helped create the polite
middle-class purlieus of Roundhay and Moortown.

The northerly sector of Leeds is hilly and abuts the great
Harewood estates. As a consequence the railway escaped to other
points of the compass. North Leeds was traditionally the place of

the polite suburbs, therefore, and long after you could go by tram
to Blackpool (all but a few miles) the northern parts of Leeds were
distinguished by their quiet and dignity and comparative wealth.
The Harewood estate prevented ribbon development along the
road to Harrogate and stopped the city at its boundary. It is a
peculiarity of Leeds that along its northern edge the break between
brick and grass is as sharp as a line drawn on a map. The outer ring
road pretty well follows this line. Beyond, the sheep and the sea-
gulls have the fields to themselves.

The first rail-commuters' suburb was at Cross Gates, which is
still Leeds busiest suburban station. Cross Gates is on the line to
York and is a pretty considerable shopping area in its own right,
as we have seen. People wanting a better deal than was available
there and unable to pay land prices in Headingley or Roundhay,
followed the train out to Ilkley, colonizing Menston, Burley and
Ben Rhydding on the way. Some Leeds businessmen and their
aspiring staff even invaded that citadel of exclusiveness, Harrogate.
Each of these places has its full complement of stone-built villas,
set in tasteful estates, their gardens shaded by proud trees planted
by grandfather in the last days of Victorian England, while
pinafored children bowled their hoops on the quiet pavements.

In this way Leeds has spread itself far beyond the city boundary.
While Leeds is a noun with a very precise meaning for its working-
class population, it is a very indefinite place-name for its richer
sons. Leeds means the city, but there are many hundreds who
work in Leeds but live outside. The Road Traffic Act of 1930
forced the competition that existed between buses and trains into
even fiercer forms. By amalgamating into larger companies, bus
undertakings were able to continue the impetus given to dispersion by the old tram. In 1921, for example, 1,858 people
worked in Leeds but lived in the urban district of Horsforth. In
1951, this figure had shown an increase of some 70 per cent.
Today Horsforth remains an urban district council whose
citizens pay rates to the West Riding; but it is in all other respects
'Leeds'. If you ask people whether they live 'in Leeds', you must
qualify this question very carefully if you are not to get the
wrong answer. At the same time, there is a pride taken in identify-
ing areas of Leeds itself not by the old postal districts, least of all
by the new postcodes, but by the old townships. There is no

confusion for those who know their 'Leeds', but plenty for those who don't—the 'incomers' who betray their foreignness by a thousand small marks of ignorance.

The commuters we have discussed so far have been the many, living in the bulk of commuter Leeds. The car—and especially 'the two-car family'—has provided the getaway people with their real getaway. Since the 'fifties, the comparatively inaccessible villages in the favoured north and east have fallen to the rich. Thorner, Bardsey, East Keswick and Collingham have some of the most expensive (and over-priced) housing in the region, with a peculiar penchant in its design for 'Georgian' windows and coachlamps over the porch. Towards the east, Boston Spa, Bramham, Sherburn and Aberford are in the same process of development. One of the by-products of this development is interesting. The ring of housing three or four miles from the city centre is respectable but very staid.

Suburban communities centre rather artificially on their churches, in imitation of ancient villages. Their pubs tend to be even more recent than their houses and serve a middle-class clientele of middle-aged folk who are hardly likely to run amok in the streets. The general atmosphere of the outlying parts of Leeds is quiet, which is why they were built, but dull. The dullness is an unfortunate side effect of suburban development, very marked in Leeds.

As a consequence, the newer commuter villages are a refuge not only to the rich industrialists and rising executives and professional men who live there, but also to the mobile middle classes who live within the city boundary. These villages have pubs which were serving ale when Roundhay was just another rocky pasture, and Moortown a windy heath with shale outcrops. The search for character and continuity is part of the reason Leeds loves its countryside. To the commuters, the exploited villages offer some sort of haven from the sheer density of the metropolitan life. To the metropolitans themselves, they represent a bit of history and a culture much older than anything they can find within the city itself.

A curious sense of pride extends to parts of Yorkshire which have as much in common with Calcutta as they have with Leeds. This pride is exercised in a very practical way. A Londoner may be able to tell where you can turn off the road to Southend for a picnic with no more than a dozen other carloads of trippers. A Leeds man will drive a hundred miles by B roads and know every pub, every view, every picnic spot and blackberry patch along the way. His relationship with the countryside environment is much more specific and determined than in many other parts of the country. He has a sense of locality—if he is a man with a car—that includes the rural parts of his county, a facet of Yorkshire life that is exceptionally significant to the planners. Yorkshire pride, of the kind that makes Yorkshire cricket and Yorkshire pudding, Yorkshire humour and Yorkshire stubbornness, is made in cities. A good Yorkshireman will let you think it is the other way around, with the Dales as the chief jewel of the county, and the cities as nothing but a blasted nuisance and excrescences on a fair rural face.

The strange love affair the city has with its rural surroundings has made the whole of Yorkshire exceptionally sensitive to planning. When one moves from the small-scale considerations of local communication, the big-time transport problems of Leeds and its region are still largely unsolved. The Leeds-Bradford Airport was set up when trams were still operating in Leeds. Its ground services were redeveloped in the late 'sixties and the hope was for a regional airport with extended runways and facilities for jet travel. The airport is not well sited, however. The objectors to the extension plans won their case in 1970, and the airport was crestfallen. In its dreams, it saw itself competing with Manchester. In reality, it was in the wrong place at the wrong time.

The loss of the air traffic at Yeadon can be offset against stream-lining of the British Rail service to London and Manchester. You can leave Leeds at 7.30 a.m. and be in London at your business meeting by half-past ten. If your business contact himself lives in London's commuter lands, he will hardly set out much later, or arrive earlier. The inter-city link to King's Cross, non-stop in under three hours makes London an easy target rather than a distant mark on the horizon. It is not unusual for those who use this train to have to explain patiently that Leeds is not at the ends of the earth, and no, they have not come down on the sleeper. The incredulity sometimes comes from 'Londoners' who live in Clacton, Cambridge, or Ramsgate—daily commuter-journeys which would be inconceivable to a Leeds man.

These pleasures are real enough, in fact they are the balancing compensation for a poor work environment for many thousands of people. From a planning point of view, the region's communications are a nightmare. The whole region is in grave danger of being split helplessly in two, the industrial conurbation falling away from the Humberside area, which has for so long depended upon its communication link with Leeds in particular.

The Yorkshire and Humberside plan published in 1966 was at any rate comprehensive. In 1970 two Hull University geographers published an exhaustive view of Humberside as a separate economic and geographic area, in which Leeds had only three passing references. A single plan for all three Ridings seems as far away as ever and part of the difficulty might be in the quality of life industrial workers are prepared to tolerate in Yorkshire for the sake of their 'independence'.

Humberside and the industrial West Riding have been connected for nearly three centuries by the Aire and Calder Navigation, the busiest canal system in England after the Manchester Ship Canal. Three and a half million tons of freight are carried each year on the Aire and Calder. The route to the deep-water estuary of the Humber has been crucial for generations. The Aire and Calder is the most important working canal system in the county. It is the only tenuous link between the industrial heart of Yorkshire and its nearest port. Humberside is standing still with only an insignificant net gain in population and without the diversity of industry to attract new capital and labour. To go to Hull is to see Leeds twenty or thirty years ago.

The number of cars on the road was trebled in the last twenty years. The effect on the urban environment of conurbated or ribbon-developed cities has been disastrous. Leeds itself has been as brutal as it dares in forcing cars out of the city centres, and making parking provisions available. But in the western approaches to Leeds the car—or rather, the road transport—has made redevelopment of small communities and townships slower and more cumbersome. The motorway city of the 'seventies has come only just in time to avert strangulation. Will the motorways now divert expenditure and planning from the places rescued? A man who has been strangled nearly to death does not recover the moment you cut the cord from his neck.

Because Yorkshire is such a vast county, peopled by some of the most sentimental patriots outside Scotland, it is able to absorb the most of bad planning and even its complete absence with something almost approaching equanimity. For example the powerful, rich and determined West Riding County Council has paid particular attention to education in the region, driven on, it is not too much of an exaggeration to say, by a brilliant Chief Education Officer and his team. The smaller county boroughs embedded in the West Riding area are too often still educational slums. The disparity of wealth, expressed as rateable value, is the lost cause of a damaging social environment. There are too many authorities, with too widely dispersed powers and too unequal resources. Sentimental pieties about Yorkshire as a whole will not suffice. Taking Yorkshire county as presently constituted, nothing but disaster surely looms ahead for its local government, a disaster hardly mitigated by good scenery and hikers' pubs. The alternative—local government reorganization—has been proposed, of course. Only Manchester United and Lancashire cricket come below it in the table of unpopularity. The argument in Leeds is an obvious one. Nothing attracts development faster in this particular phase of the industrial revolution than the material welfare a city can offer its inhabitants, both to keep its own labour force and attract the fast-growth new firms and their staffs. Leeds has turned itself inside out in an attempt to increase the net product of material benefits like housing, welfare, education, public services and inducements to private enterprise. Nevertheless its population is comparatively static. It is only just breaking out of its old reputation as a dirty, sooty place to live. It has overcome the legacies of the past: but only quite recently.

There is an argument that says local government reorganization (which would spread Leeds along its North–West axis deep into the West Riding) would produce that increase of population and rateable wealth which would spur its economy on. It seems doubtful. The easiest way out of the dilemma and one which is constantly harped on, is to accept the difficulties but claim the countryside as a playground and as a natural extension of the city environment. Leeds, which was once the envy of the textile world now employs only one man in fifty in its production (leaving tailoring out of it altogether). In the textile towns that neighbour it, 20 per cent of the working population works at the loom. These towns are dependent on Leeds in a dozen different ways, quite apart from the sale of their cloth. It seems a curious and in some ways unworthy compliment to lump all together in one romantic binge on Cup Final day or at the Test ground in Headingley. Leeds holds the key to any major regional redevelopment. When it comes the poetry of a sunset over Pen-y-Ghent will not answer to the problems reorganization creates. In the early days of trams, where Leeds met Bradford at Stanningley, the gauge of the tracks altered, "as surely", as a Professor of Economics has put it, "as at any Russian border". The county council and the ten county boroughs are not a great deal further forward with today's problems.

XV

THE FUTURE

SINCE this is not a history proper of Leeds (for that has yet to be written) but a more subjective account, it should be possible to begin to draw together some strands into a convincing portrait. The underpainting that is the first task of the portraitist is something it takes him a lifetime to learn. By comparison, this portrait is painted with colour straight from the tube. Yet there are some general points which are worth re-emphasizing about the ground we have covered.

The feeling of density a townscape has is for the people who live there something very deep within their consciousness. They grow up with a visual store of information that has right at the heart the crowded quality of the streets they live in. The old butchers' shambles about Briggate have long since gone, but they are not the only image by which density of environment is conveyed. Narrow streets and overhanging eaves are only one version of a town's crowded existence. Huddled houses and scribbled streets have a fascination which is for us historical. There are none left in Leeds. The feeling of density is no less apparent.

It is one quality mixed with another. Leeds has the feel of a big city—a vast tract of housing, many thousands of people; but set in some sort of regularity. Density and regularity march in step. Maybe incorporation in 1835 set this march in progress and removed the clustering hive around Briggate. Regularity as much as overcrowding is the feeling in the remaining back-to-back terraces. These steep streets of back-to-backs are all the more depressing for being so regular.

In some ways the effect is that of an unemotional, heartless kind of planning, only partly saved by the improvised community that is made in the densely packed homes. Hunslet had its own

particular character, but that Hunslet is as good as gone. Chapeltown perhaps never truly had an idiosyncratic life of its own, of
the outward-going cheerful, hearty kind we admire in men. The
immigrants who moved to Chapeltown from the Leylands
built regularity and nondescriptness into their housing. After
all, why not? That regular, orderly development is something
that the West Indians who took over the district have not been
able to alter in any substantial way. Again, why should they?

The massive municipalization of housing has likewise mixed the
feel of a big city with regular, orderly development. In planning
terms, these are positive virtues. They are extremely depressing
when the development is finally laid out. The Belle Isle estate is an
example of housing where hundreds of acres look the same,
express the same careful reticence, and create for the people who
live there an environment which may be safe, but in time stunts
rather than shapes personality. While Leeds is in many ways a
city of optimum size, not so small that its interests are parochial,
not so large that it swamps all individuality, it shares with big
cities the world over that loss of character which makes some
places hell on earth. The problem of human relationships. A mass
is not a family, nor is it a clan. A hundred clubs, two hundred
societies do not break down a mass into manageable proportions.
What does we have yet to find out.

Leeds is by no means a tidy city. So much of it is being changed
so suddenly that it is sometimes more like a vast builder's yard
than a spruce civic enterprise. There are a good many mysterious
spaces left undeveloped and barren quite close to the city centre
and a good number of streets that are scheduled for destruction
living out their lease on life in an elderly untidiness. At the same
time, no one who has lived in Leeds long can ignore the sense of
order imposed by conflicting interests and at different periods of
history. The effect is a curious one. Leeds is quite clearly a very
large city to anyone finding his way around, but it is at the same
time a curiously deserted place. This is especially so at night.

No one in their right mind would come to Leeds for profligacy
or sin, although both obviously exist. After the war, Leeds was
notorious for its prostitution and crime, a situation reversed by
the sterling actions of a vigorous chief constable. The subsequent
improvement in public morals was no doubt a great blessing to all

save the girls who were turfed out of their pitches on Bond Street and Commercial Street; but with them may have gone the only real anti-city that could have developed in Leeds.

These indelicate matters have their place. It may well be that the idea of an organic community the size of Leeds is an impossibility. Cities might once have had a single, corporate life, but no longer. Perhaps the Royal visit of 1858 was the last great occasion when all were one in a beery, patriotic, sentimental family. Certainly it is difficult to point to any one circumstance or event which would identify Leeds as a separate, special place, even for the people who live there. Leeds is much more a generalized concept place name in inverted commas, it is the city, but it also is the commuter villages and the region as well. It has four Members of Parliament and eleven ancient townships, an ancient parish church and a hundred chapels, a dozen millionaires and a couple of thousand unemployed. Never mind the remainder of the big city; if the people did not go straight home and stay put, we would be in trouble. It is a city; but it is also a dormitory.

An anti-city is a tempting idea, something to harass the planners with. One of the most subtle changes to have come over Leeds might turn out to be its progressive conversion to middle-class standards of manners and behaviour. Leeds is not a great working-class citadel. The reforming zeal of the last hundred years has softened Leeds up for the comfy, cosy, accepting world of the compromise and the conforming reconciliation of differences. It would be ludicrous to say that any one part of Leeds is like any other, although much more arguable that within kinds of community this is so. Headingley is still remote from Hunslet, yet not altogether different from Roundhay. Middleton and Gipton were created at the same time, by the same rehousing scheme. They have few marked differences of character.

The materials for an anti-city are lying about to hand. The historic division into separate 'townships' is the most obvious. Seacroft New Town is hardly the model. But what if Wortley and Holbeck, even lofty Headingley and remote Adel were to 'secede' from Leeds? Just because the area of the city in acres is so vast, the possibility of a great reversionary development into local communities is more possible. It is a very significant fact that no district of Leeds is without its own extensive public park. One of the smaller pleasures of living there is the comparatively luxurious provision of open space, breaking up the regularity of the city with some feeling of locality.

The public parks in Leeds are of potentially vital significance in the future of Leeds. Partly by accident, partly by design, the city has increased its two historic open spaces—Woodhouse and Holbeck Moor—to a really substantial green-space provision. A park in Leeds is no new football pitch with a show of salvias or geraniums in season. The biggest is of course Roundhay, which has not one but two lakes, a forest of rhododendrons and enough open ground to be called parkland more than park. The acquisition of Roundhay Park was a piece of gifted municipal long-sightedness to be set alongside the purchase of Temple Newsam.

Leeds parks are big places and they are interesting places. They offer real alternatives to the housing, not just tokens. Ornithologists and botanists can get a good education from Leeds parks by examining the areas left untouched by the gardeners. You could even say that the parks convey a feeling of freedom from planning that is otherwise rare. (For this it may be more exact to thank subtle parks government rather than mere chance.) For example, when Woodhouse Moor was laid out to walks and avenues in the 1840s, part of it to the east was left as wild moorland. Although the smaller parks can hardly emulate this, where there is the possibility of 'natural' development this has been subtly preserved, as at Becketts Park and even Harehills. Most Leeds parks are heavily wooded.

A parks culture in Leeds would be a fine thing. Perhaps the newly appointed community development officers for the city could do worse than develop a 'people and parks' policy, using the one obvious and available locale in each area which has none of the daunting regularity of the streets themselves. Perhaps street-theatre (of which there are at least two Leeds troupes) could become parks theatre. In the summer perhaps much much more could be done to get children involved in activities centred on these invaluable park lands of the city.

The city needs to have its anti-city for its future health. A good deal of the best in Leeds is explained by negative emphasis—no more slums, no more congestion, no more traffic chaos, no more vice and crime. Even if these negatives are wholly true of Leeds, they require opposing positives of a kind that the community itself will have to find. As we have seen with Seacroft the new does not by itself remove problems—it simply restates the problems in a different context. When so much of Leeds is new (and so much is) the weathering of the stone will need to be helped along, not left to vagary or Leeds weather.

There are some powerful new ingredients to reckon with in Leeds life. At the end of its first half-century the university was comfortably assured of its place in the city and quietly indulgent of its educational role. The very rapid explosion of university education in the last twenty years has ended all that. The development plan for the university, now nearing its fulfilment, has finally extinguished the last of the Beech Grove calm and quiet. Leeds now has one of the most dramatic university developments this country has ever seen.

Durham is a good example of what an ancient university can do to increase its capacity while retaining its original character. York is an example of what can be borrowed locally by an entirely new foundation. (The university acquired the exquisite Mansion House as its city-centre headquarters, while building the main blocks outside the boundaries.) Leeds, by comparison, is an example of a university within a city that now completely dominates its original site.

The Portland stone and solemn awe of the Parkinson Building is now only the small outward sign of what has become in effect a city within a city. It is not clear whether Leeds completely understands what a colossal actual change of landscape has occurred on the university site. By the time the access roads and peripheral building is complete, the university will be seen in its true perspective, as a knowledge factory which could put Bean Ing Mills and Marshall's Flax Mill into its pocket and not show the bulge. Its scale is titantic, in fact the main spine bears an uncanny resemblance to an ocean-going liner, stranded by some receding tide on the slope of land which rises up behind the town hall.

The knowledge industry in Leeds is the last long-overdue phase of industrial revolution. The university and the newly designated polytechnic touch fingers across the inner ring road and each cruises down the hill to the great teaching hospital of the General

Infirmary. That sector of the city to the north of the Headrow and east of Woodhouse Lane is in scale as big as anything ever accomplished in a comparable period in Leeds. It overlooks Barran's original factory. The development from that enterprise has been incalculable. Can one any better quantify the effect on Leeds of its new-scale university?

Until the recent past, a university has in its own keeping the sort of image it wished to create. An admissions policy could be (and often was) quirky. Its teaching was similarly idiosyncratic. Academic appointments—indeed whole university departments —flourished (or did not) according to something which when it worked was ascribed to genius. When it didn't work it was put down to a fact of nature—"this university is not particularly interested in your subject or your area of research". Sometimes, even "we don't do that here".

University professors are not public servants in the same way that principals or headmasters are. Until recently, again, the function of the university as a teaching agency was variously interpreted, from one university to another and within individual faculties of a particular university. The curious status of universities is reflected in the collegiate examples, particularly Oxford and Cambridge. The buildings are clearly private buildings with the privileges of private foundations, yet they are at the same time the place of public education for the majority of those who are selected to live and work there. The county council may send your son there on a grant, but the college will retain its private character unaltered. If your son turns out to be a waste of public money, it will be behind the sheltered walls of an ancient, honourable and independent foundation.

In practice this system of university education has proved extremely efficient. Universities need academic independence which they can only get from the principle of (comparative) constitutional and governmental independence. While it was quite clear in the recent past that fewer men and women received a university education than could benefit by it, at the same time the universities retained a very high standard of academic freedom and were able to assert standards of enquiry and debate which drew their strength from a privileged objectivity. The dons and the public servants in Whitehall and the county Education

Officer made an elegant and thoroughly English compromise of interests.

The rapid growth of higher education has changed much, nowhere faster than at Leeds. Leeds is now a university which is geared to mass production, just as are all the rest. Its admissions policy, the balance of power within the faculties, its building programme and capital investment are still in the hands of its own chartered servants, but very far removed from the days when Vice-Chancellor Baillie won financial security and academic freedom by dining at the tables of the rich. Its 'public' character, in other words, has immeasurably increased. As a centre for higher education and a statistic of educational opportunity, Leeds has its place in a national picture of growth, greatly increased public investment, and increasing political involvement in education.

The architecture of the new buildings is dramatic and sudden. The site occupies a hill, so that the main teaching block is on several levels. Coloured routes guide you as you go and there is even a perpetual lift into which you post yourself like a parcel in a sorting office, jumping out when you reach the right floor. Everything about the buildings and their environments suggests size, and speed. The calm, studied exteriors of the Parkinson with their lofty ceilings and measured pillars have given way to the new material, concrete. The effect is to give a restatement of purpose to every aspect of the campus. Nothing suggests expediency and speed better than concrete—fast building for fast living.

Just how fast the living will be is the question. In 1874 the Yorkshire College opened in a forsaken bankruptcy court with a single student. In the next ten years perhaps 50,000 young men and women will be drafted into the great complicated machine its successor has become. The new university is like a machine whose working parts are human. Once set in motion it requires those human parts in a regular flow. Like a machine, it has had cost-efficiency written into it. Again, like a machine, there is a limit to the amount of sentiment which can be expended. You get nowhere talking to a typewriter. A typewriter is for a specific use.

But much more than a single machine, the university is an undertaking of industrial proportions. Will there be a spin-off? In short, could the university teach the city how to live? The answer rests not with the staff but with the student body. Leeds desperately needs young initiative. We have seen how it was founded on the enterprise of young men, men at the very outset of their working life. The extra-mural contract of the university with the city is not particularly strong at student level. But the original intention of the ancient universities was not to remove them from workaday life, but to place them at the centre. Oxford and Cambridge were good sites for universities because those towns were good strong markets. Is there any comparison to be made with the situation as it is now in Leeds?

The anti-city will need to arise within the city itself. The pleasure urban Yorkshire takes in the surrounding countryside is only a partial solution to its urban problems. Towns that are a lot smaller than Leeds have fewer problems. Only half a dozen cities in England have Leeds's problems. As we have seen, Leeds is a new town that has taken 150 years to build. It is no solution to its future development to point north to the Dales or east to the coast and direct its re-creative energies outwards. You get little new in a city from a people who are constantly leaving it to restore their sanity and health.

If Leeds is to become a motorway city of the 'seventies, will it be nothing more than the largest service station and lay-by the world has ever seen, or will it be that rare, rare phenomenon— a city of half a million or more of population that is a tolerable environment and an exciting place to live? If it tries for the latter, a good many of its traditional virtues will have to be given radical reconsideration. Leeds has survived a pretty cataclysmic recent history by silent virtues of the kind much admired in Yorkshire as a whole—thrift, prudence, industry, chapel rectitude. By such a drastic change in its environment it has willy-nilly changed the man. How much further he will change is a question hanging in the air not only for Leeds for the whole of urban Britain. The lines of experience written across any portrait of Leeds are not those of an old man, but of a man in his prime. But to pick up the opportunity that at last presents itself to a majority of the city's people, after so long and so dour a battle, will need more grit, more determination, more enterprise than ever before. It is not that enough has not been done. It is that the new game is only just about to start.

XVI

CONCLUSIONS AND NEW BEGINNINGS

W E   C A N begin to draw together a composite portrait of a Leeds citizen from what has been said about his city. The exercise is full of dangers, but valuable. The dangers are that the real idiosyncrasy, such as you get with individual people (a sudden smile, a sudden fit of rage) is smoothed out in any general account. The value is in the questions raised. For example, we can say with some certainty that the Leeds man is smaller than his cousin in the South. There was a time when he was worse nourished, and with a lower expectancy of life. His earnings are still lower than many of his friends with comparable skills in a city like Birmingham. Apart from a few experiments, the car industry is one which never took root in Leeds, and the city has never attracted it. As big-spending high-wage aggressive workers, carworkers are completely foreign to industrial experience in Leeds.

Our composite citizen is a cautious man. He has not known the bonanza times of other cities, or other industries, but neither has he known the starkest depressions. He knows he has a range of jobs and trades in which to raise his children, and he has some confidence in their prospects. He knows that he is an important factor in the region's life, for he can see at a glance that while the *Yorkshire Post* may be for folk he is not likely to meet, the *Evening Post* is a great national evening paper expressly catering for his interest and his taste. He can see that the same is true of the local radio station and to a great extent Yorkshire Television. Opinion-making in Leeds starts from the shop-floor and the council estate. When his daughter marries and moves away to the South, he will go to visit her and marvel at the strange sort of news they put in the papers down there, all of doings that could not possibly interest him.

He is a kind man, by and large. His caution with money and

property has made him to some extent reticent and shy. He has what some folk would call a bit of an inferiority complex, even. But although he knows he lives in a male-orientated society, he has a kindness and tolerance all of his own. He would be embarrassed to have that pointed out to him too often. About some things he is stubborn. His pride is reserved for who he is when he's at home. It's a matter of pride with him to do his own repairs, take an interest in his own car, dig his bit of garden unaided, get by without fuss. He dislikes fuss and emotional things and his sense of humour is of a piece with this—laconic and dry.

He likes his pint, sport, and in a strange way work itself. Londoners probably strike him as being too big for their boots, and with too much mouth for his taste. He's not completely dutiful, completely subservient to the boss, but he turns in a day's work for a day's pay. He likes to see a result from what he does. He doesn't live to work, but he respects work. It has been part of his heritage. There is some work that is meaningless to him— for example the sort of life the hill farmers lead in their lonely houses forty or so miles from his front door. But at the same time he has not been completely dissociated from the life work creates. He is proud of the works team, honoured by the firm's awards to long-serving members, tickled pink by working for a firm with a long tradition behind it. Unusual work—such as that done by artists, or picture-restorers, or cathedral masons—intrigues him.

Our composite man is probably in his middle years. Leeds has never been a city of greybeards but it has lost some of its youthful zest. The middle-of-the-road opinion is also middle-aged in character and this mature, reflective unexcited quality our composite man will pass on to his children. He is proportionately baffled by the youth revolution, long hair, hippie clothes and such like. He sees all that sort of thing as an intrusion, just as anything new strikes him as odd. He is a traditionalist with only a few traditions immediately to hand. He likes anything that is old and has an interest in history, of the sort you can go and see, that is remarkable. If he is not very open-minded at times, you have to remember that his grandfather clung on to Leeds for his very life. Open-mindedness is all very well, but what our man has won for himself has not been without struggle. Too much that is new, too much that is alien to what went before, makes him uneasy.

This sort of man is, he well knows, half the population of Leeds. In the region as a whole, he is in the majority. He has no experience of an army of clerks and office workers moving in and out of his streets daily. He knows Leeds is the regional capital in all but name, but he knows too that its claims to such depend upon him. He is an ordinary sort of man with very ordinary ambitions. He senses from the postal frank on his letters, proclaiming a motorway city, that something is going to be asked of him soon. Indeed, it will be remarkable if change has not already touched him quite hard. He is likely to be living in a newish house, or with the threat of demolition hanging over his old house. His children have, as he always wanted, a better chance in life, so far as education goes, than he had himself. The centre of his city, where he will sometimes take the wife shopping, is changing almost daily.

He is an average of all the conditions that act upon a great city like Leeds. If he is reading this page, he will disagree wholeheartedly with every characteristic given him. But one thing does mark him out. Whatever his little idiosyncrasies, however he wriggles out of the general description given above, he is a man likely to stay put in Leeds. The population of Leeds has advanced by about 100,000 this century. In the first seventy years of last century, three times as many flocked to Leeds. The great explosion has rumbled now to a comparative silence and the storms that it produced have ended. The net gain in population for the whole region is virtually at a standstill. The people who have made Leeds are the people who will stay to finish the job. Even if our man has never heard of Samuel Smiles and the doctrine of self-help, he will know that whatever is going to get done in Leeds will not depend on a sudden new inrush of strangers. He can expect no dramatic new industrial developments and no startling rise in wages. A Leeds man is luckier than many in the North, as he well realizes. At the emotional level, he had better think well of his home town, because he has been born to stay.

What sort of future will he find for himself? In the proposals for local government reorganization, Leeds will become one of four major units of government carved from the historic West

Riding. A great draught of air will flow in where the knife has cut. The current proposals for reorganization will dismember the West Riding County Council's epoch-making adventure in education and give away at least some of the disciplined power that created in the industrial parts of Yorkshire a social concern expressed through education that has had few parallels in Britain.

In this cutting of a truly stupendous cake, Leeds will gain in size and influence. Its territorial advantage will then run roughly with its present influence. The new Leeds will extend far beyond the county borough boundaries, and far beyond the concept of a county borough. The chartered city will not disappear; of course it will not. But the idea of a contained entity, a single unit, however complex, which can own to the name of Leeds will necessarily disappear. The next book on Leeds may well not start with a train ride into the station built so cunningly across the Aire, but by an aerial view of the new Leeds, a great city *and* a great fan-shaped wedge of countryside, dotted with smaller towns, villages, outlying farms and open moorland.

It is beyond the scope of this book to analyse the effect on Leeds as an industrial and commercial unit. It is well within the scope to ask what will become of the essential community founded on a crossing of a river, as so many towns have been founded. And to do this, we have to go back again to the origins of the city.

For so many years Leeds was Briggate, the road leading up from the bridge. Even before there was the most elementary kind of bridge there, the path existed. From that one axis, the whole of Leeds has developed and to stand in Briggate today is to stand at the heart of its history. We have seen how in the eighteenth century, for all its wealth and population, Leeds as a set of buildings was hardly much more than you could get into an 80-acre field. Briggate was the spine of that development too. We have seen how the town grew in the nineteenth century, the becks filling with housing until they were completely paved from the ridge to the Aire itself. Still Briggate was the core of the sprawling red manufacturing town beginning to alarm the rest of the country.

This town, the new town, which was set down with as much emphasis as an alien culture, something from another world, writhed and grew wherever resistance was least. Like an alien growth, it seeded itself, ran away with land, tore deep into the old Domesday townships held by the seven thanes of Edward the Confessor. It encircled them, strangled some, brought others back from the dead. When cheap transport came, the growth was more rational and showed a greater order and purpose. Yet still no one suburb of Leeds was able to run away completely from the original site of community. We have seen how, in post-war years, it has even been possible to create a new town within a new town and still have room and enough for the idea of one Leeds, indivisible. Whatever happens to Seacroft, we can be certain that it will remain Leeds, always Leeds. The town centre at Seacroft cost over £2 million, and is practically deserted. Briggate, or the Leeds symbolized in Briggate, is infinitely more powerful.

In this one respect, Leeds is like a village of enormous size. You are either in Leeds or you are not. In Cambridge, you can live your whole life in the Mill Road area, or out Chesterton way, and know that the Backs exist, yet never go there. You can do a full day's shopping in Cambridge and walk a couple of miles and never bother to look in through the gates of a college. Many Cambridge people do just that. It is as though a part of the city—for visitors the only interesting part—is for the people who live there completely unconsidered. There are special reasons for this, but the comparison points up a quality of Leeds life that is remarkable. Leeds is a very large city indeed, in acreage, yet it is all Leeds. In other words, the Hunslet man and the Seacroft man have in their bones a feeling for Leeds. They may not exactly know just what they mean by the word, but they feel it. The place is huge, but it is all one community.

The reorganization of local government, which will give the city a broad inverted wedge of the county, must destroy that community of interests and emotional identity. Reorganization will mean the collapse of the historic architecture of sentiment and affection which has been built on the slow and steady slope of Briggate. For the folk who are to be brought into the new authority, there is, at any rate in principle, nothing but good to come from reorganization. In theory, their government will become more local and their opportunity for participation more immediate. Their political interests will be realigned along the path of their commercial appetites—if they shop in Leeds, they will pay rates there, elect their representative within the town hall (the town hall?) and consider themselves Leeds Loiners. All this is in theory, alas. For part of the new Leeds would be the old Harrogate. One need hardly go further in argument. Leeds is so emphatically not Harrogate that only Whitehall could have dreamed up that grotesque adoption.

For the Leeds of this book, too, the reorganization would spell a defeat just at the very moment when some sort of victory was to be wrung from a long and arduous struggle. Leeds has its own identity, jealously guarded, won with honour. Changes in local government are not simply administrative conveniences. They are fire to the flimsy materials of pride of place, confidence in the community, respect and affection. Our composite Leeds citizen has been moulded from forces which at first denied him his place in English society and then helped him build that society over anew. His city is in his image. There are no flamboyant parts to its story, no great and stirring battles, no castle sieges or Tudor pageantry. It is a workaday city with a character that is enigmatic. Like its average citizen, Leeds is hard-bitten. It has had its historians. Now it needs its poet.

INDEX

A

B